SIMPLE RULES:

A RADICAL INQUIRY INTO SELF

In praise of

Simple Rules:
A Radical Inquiry
into Self

This is a clear, straight-forward approach to one of the most significant organizing principles in the dynamics of human systems. Royce Holladay and Mallary Tytel share their rich experience and insights bravely and generously. I can't wait to use this promising practical guide to revisit my own simple rules, and recommend others to do the same.

Dr. Judy Meisels Tal,
Principle, LearningCycles

The genius of the authors is that they have conveyed what is expected and demanded of those seeking lasting change. **Simple Rules** *is a wonderfully written explanation of how the smallest changes can profoundly impact the world. This is a book with universal appeal and application for personal and organizational success.*

Timothy Germany,
Commissioner,
Federal Mediation and Conciliation Service

This succinct volume uses simple stories and metaphors to help us recognize the patterns we act out on a daily basis. It then gives us specific ways to create new, empowering methods to think and act. **Simple Rules** *allowed me to see where my means of operating helped me meet my goals and where I needed to change my patterns to get back on track. I can use it for myself and apply it to organizations. There is lots of impact here in a few pages!*

Katherine Barton,
Consultant, Educator, Community Volunteer

We live in a world that is increasingly connected. Opportunities to optimize our human potential are everywhere. We can make new connections and influence those around us positively every day, and in so doing improve our own capabilities. All we have to do is to decide how we want that to happen. It's up to us now to channel that potential, that best of who we are, toward the greatest challenge facing humanity: that of achieving global sustainability on our shared planet.

Simple Rules *helps lead us toward coherence in attitude and behavior and thereby the confidence that our emerging positive purpose will be present in our every interaction.*

Dr. Enrico Wensing,
Founder of Ecosphere Net
Author of *I Am Sustainability*

Also by Royce Holladay

Legacy: Sustainability in a Complex Human System

Co-authored with Kristine Quade

Influencing Patterns for Change: A Human Systems Dynamics Primer for Leaders

Dynamical Leadership: Building Adaptive Capacity for Uncertain Times

Also by Mallary Tytel

Vision Driven: Lessons Learned from the Small Business C-Suite

SIMPLE RULES:

A RADICAL INQUIRY INTO SELF

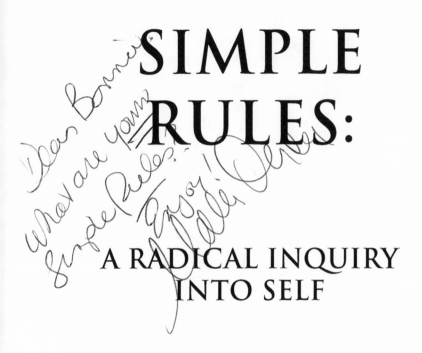

GOING BEYOND SELF-HELP TO GENERATE SELF-HOPE

ROYCE HOLLADAY
MALLARY TYTEL

Gold Canyon Press

To contact the authors with comments or to inquire about speaking, coaching or consulting, you may write to them at
 Royce@simplerules.org or Mallary@simplerules.org

Please be sure to visit the Simple Rules Foundation at www.simplerulesfoundation.org

---

Simple Rules:
A Radical Inquiry into Self

Gold Canyon Press
P.O. Box 2223
Apache Junction, Arizona 85217-2223
U.S.A.

www.goldcanyonpress.com
www.simplerules.org

PB ISBN: 978-0-9821112-2-2
PRINTED IN THE UNITED STATES OF AMERICA

CONTENTS

Acknowledgments

With great appreciation and affection we recognize and express our thanks to individuals who provided their time, energy, wisdom, and support to help make this book a reality.

- **Glenda Eoyang,** Executive Director of Human Systems Dynamics Institute, who got this all started and encouraged us throughout the process.

- **Mary Nations,** Principal of Nations Alliance in Raleigh, NC, and Human Systems Dynamics Institute Associate. Her reading and thoughtful feedback proved invaluable in helping us clarify concepts as we told the story of radical inquiry.

- **Jessica Tytel,** MPH, Office of the Assistant Secretary for Preparedness and Response, U.S. Department of Health and Human Services, who read, reviewed, and provided wonderful feedback that helped us clarify our language and messages about Radical Inquiry.

- **Bradley Tytel,** Director, Global Health Strategies, who created magic with his ideas, talents and graphic mastery.

Royce acknowledges her amazing daughters, Toni Martinez and Tori Chandler, for unflagging support, encouragement, and patience as she has grown through her own Radical Inquiry. She also thanks Jo Klemm and Leslie Patterson, who both continue to support this work in creative ways. And as always— thanks to Glenda, for teaching and learning in every interaction.

Mallary wants to recognize and thank her family, Stephen, Jess, and Brad, who support and contribute to the patterns of her life. She would also like to extend her gratitude and deep appreciation to Glenda Eoyang, for sustaining the effort ... and granola.

FOREWORD

I have found middle age to be shockingly similar to adolescence. My body is changing. My roles and responsibilities are new. My relationships with others become deeper and more complex as they mature. At fourteen, I expected transformation. I'd read Catcher in the Rye, Little Women, and Arthurian legends so I had some idea about what it meant to come of age. The future was full of promise, and I was excited to meet it with open arms and open heart.

Fifty-five, on the other hand, brings me into uncharted and distressing territory. Parents and friends don't talk about it much except to condemn someone else's "midlife crisis." Literature paints a picture of disappointment and longing. Advertising promises challenges we can hardly imagine for our grandparents, much less for ourselves. None of this reflects my own experiences of expanding community, exploding learning, and deep satisfaction that have come with aging. None of these supports me in my daily striving for learning and life. As the Baby Boom generation moves into and through our middle years, we need ways to see and celebrate the emergent patterns in our maturing selves. I believe this book shines a light on those patterns and provides a simple way to engage with the complexities of life—early, middle, and late.

Usually self-help books either tell you how to come to terms with yourself or how to reshape your relationships with others. Royce and Mallary have chosen a third path that lies at the intersections of self and other; thought, emotion, and action; past, present, and future. Their approach is based on my work in human systems dynamics; and my work is based on synergies between social sciences and the emerging new sciences of chaos and complexity. We all owe enormous debts to the researchers and inventors who have informed us. More importantly, though, we recognize that our work is informed by our practice. Every single day, we engage with ourselves in inquiry to resolve underlying tensions that separate us from our real selves and our deepest happiness. We live with nuclear and extended families who challenge us to engage with clarity and courage. We also enter the world as professionals to see and influence patterns, productivity, and satisfaction for individuals, teams, and organizations. All of these situations are full of potential for learning. Everyone invites us to actualize our unique opportunities.

As we observe ourselves and others, we know that our work is equally informed by internal and external engagements, by reflection and action, and by individual and collective inquiry. This book demonstrates all of those complex relationships in a simple and accessible way. No mystery here, no guru on the hill, no arrogant assumption of spiritual enlightenment, only simple and powerful questions and the transformations they spark.

Nonlinear dynamics, including chaos and complexity sciences, can push the bounds of understanding, even for the most curious layperson. Butterfly effects, strange attractors, fractals, tipping points, emergence have all entered the garden variety vocabulary since the mid-90s. Unfortunately, though, the underlying theory about what drives complex adaptive systems remains a mystery to most people. Many of the methods and tools that are used to observe, understand, and manage complex dynamics are even more difficult to master. While everyone knows that the world is becoming more complex, few are able to engage with that complexity in generative and productive ways. Human systems dynamics, and its network of certified professionals, strive to bring complexity down to earth and put it into the hands of real people doing real work. In Simple Rules, Royce and Mallary do just that. They take an incredibly complex challenge—finding hope in the midst of uncertainty. They introduce a powerful and simple tool to address that challenge—simple rules. And they present that tool, and its various uses, in language that is engaging and accessible. The result, as you will see, unfolds into a new way to engage with yourself and others to maximize your learning and happiness in the midst of an uncertain future.

As I read the book, I recognized myself at my most successful and satisfying moments. Those moments occur invariably when I am engaged in meaningful inquiry. Simple Rules outlines the practical tools and methods that make it easier to be curious and practical. It provides the tools I need to navigate unknown terrain, including the fascinating journey of middle age. I commend this book to you and hope that you find these and other theories and tools of human systems dynamics to empower and enrich your life.

~Glenda Eoyang
Circle Pines, Minnesota USA
August 26, 2010

INTRODUCTION

In ancient times signal lights were used to mark the path for returning travelers and to warn distant communities of approaching danger. Huge bonfires were built in relay, with each distant fire just barely visible to the next posted watcher. Upon sighting the distant blaze, the watcher then lit his fire, to be seen by the next watcher, at the third post, who lit his fire to be seen by a fourth watcher. This series of fires formed a continuous line of connections, safely guiding travelers into unfamiliar territory or marking the passage of news and information across vast distances.

This metaphor gives a rich image for how individuals and groups learn to explore the depths of who they are, what they want, and how they take action to move forward. Individuals come to points in their lives where they enter new and—for them— uncharted territory. The only way forward is to ask questions—seek meaning—in the context of that new environment. People ask questions of themselves; they ask questions of others; and they ask about the meaning of what they see in their worlds. These questions are like signal fires, helping individuals see and make meaning of their immediate space, even as they move toward the next place of unknown and confusion, where the next question lights their way.

We think of each signal fire as a set of major questions human beings ask themselves as they move forward. As they pass through their current stages of life, with whatever challenges, joys, relationships, or accomplishments it brings, they know the inevitability of change. They know that as they age—as they learn, as they move in any direction—they will change. If they continue to ask significant questions about their lives and themselves, their paths will be illuminated by the learning and insights those questions bring.

Chapter 1

"Situational variables can exert powerful influences over human behavior, more so than we recognize or acknowledge."

~Philip Zimbardo

This quote speaks to the heart of what this chapter is about. Human systems dynamics focuses on human behavior and the forces— both internal and external to the individual— that shape their minute-by-minute decisions about how they live, work, and play together.

Dive into this chapter to learn about four major concepts that will become critical to your discovery of self-hope.

Simple Rules

Set against the backdrop of today's challenging and complex world, there is something inside individuals that drives what they do. When they were young and dependent on the wisdom and actions of people around them, they watched what others did, how people fared in their actions and seemed to make their decisions.

Early in life individuals decide whether the ways others live make sense to them. They don't know at the time, but they are, in fact, lighting those very first signal fires for themselves; using questions to light their own paths and choice.

- Who or what could be trusted?

- What could or should be tolerated in life?

- What is the meaning of work and community?

- What is important?

As they answered those earliest questions for themselves, they formed values and beliefs that helped them light their own paths in that portion of their world and in that segment of their lives. In this way, they learned to survive however they could. These values became the ground upon which they built the paths of their lives and the foundations for all future questions.

These types of questions formulate foundational values and world views. For some, these early-formed values generated a set of precepts, or rules for living, which then remained embedded as they matured, continuing to guide their individual journeys. Their signal fires are driven by questions about how best to maintain today's reality and today's position in life.

Others use those early-formed values as a springboard to search for infinite possibilities that lie just out of sight. They seek questions that will light the next fire, drawing them toward the next possibility. Their signal fires are driven by questions about how best to seek new challenges and experiences.

Some individuals follow signal fires that guide them to raise families and continue to prosper in their hometown communities. Others follow signal fires that guide them to return to school for further education, greater knowledge, and higher degrees. Creative individuals pursue fires that take them to fine, performing, and interpretive arts. Individuals become politically active or work to pursue their passions—civil rights, peace, universal health, sustainability and global warming, family interests, entrepreneurship, or spiritual enlightenment.

Some people build their lives by settling down in one place and into a routine they maintain across all their adult years. Occasional outliers may settle down until in midlife, they sell everything they own, buy an RV, and take to a vagabond existence on the road. People, in their own individual ways, endeavor to make sense of the world, to have their voices heard, and to make their choices known. Each human moves toward the next signal fire's set of questions, building the path that is his or her life.

"Human behavior flows from three main sources:
desire, emotion and knowledge."
~Plato

The foundation that lights the paths of human growth emerge from inquiry into Plato's sources. Each person asks some form of these questions.

- What do I want?

- How do I feel?

- What do I know?

Multiple and varied answers mark life paths as individuals establish patterns of action and thought that characterize their existence and influence their next decisions.

We have been thinking about this, too, and we believe we have found a way to think about those questions in ways that help us be more intentional about our own paths. Part of our own discovery has been to confront and test our assumptions and theories about the world and ourselves. What we have found is this.

- The boundaries we create for ourselves not only separate us from others, they also connect us to others in some cases.

- The ideas and issues that are important to us are both personal and universal in our worlds. What makes a difference to us, individually, also matters in some ways as we participate in our families, communities, and ultimately as we take our places as members of the greater global community.

- We interact with others according to a personal set of principles or rules that create a framework for measuring everything else. These rules provide us with a coherent strand of straightforward and uncomplicated instructions about life. In other

words, each individual functions according to a short list of simple rules.

> **Simple:** plain, basic, uncomplicated in form.
>
> **Simple Rules** provide plain, basic, uncomplicated set of guidelines for living your life.

Let us introduce you to what we mean by the notion of simple rules. Simple rules are those specific, uncomplicated instructions that guide behavior and create the structure within which human beings can live their lives. They come from an individual's beliefs, values, and understandings about the world. They allow people to create the context for how they function—how they show the world what they value and understand. Simple rules generate the questions that light the signal fires as people find their ways in life.

Even when an individual is unaware of the presence and impact of his or her own short list of simple rules, they are there. The list forms the basis for the larger dialogue individuals have with the world, guiding their everyday journeys, and pointing the way for moving forward. Simple rules do this by informing people's choices in various areas across their lives. This short list creates consistency and coherence that build familiarity—they create patterns that come to characterize peoples' lives.

Patterns of Life

Look around you. Your life is made up of complex patterns. For example, is there ever enough time, money, fun, and satisfaction for you? Who are the carpoolers and who are the walkers? What does the book club read and why? Who volunteers at school, and who can you count on for the latest piece of neighborhood gossip? Do you feel rushed and harried throughout most of your day, or do you regularly manage a chunk of quality time for yourself to put your feet up, read today's paper today, and gently nod off before duty calls once again?

If you pay attention, you will notice patterns in the recognizable and repeated ways your life is similar from one day to the next. Patterns are those experiences that set you apart from others in day-to-day interactions; and they are the threads of relationships that make up the tapestries of your life. Thoughtful, curious, and deliberate individuals are driven to make sense of their patterns and how they can influence them.

What many people don't know is that they have choices about what patterns they live with and which ones they can eliminate from their lives. They have a choice about generating new patterns that enrich and fulfill their lives. They have a choice to build patterns that create a pathway to peace of mind—or not. Individuals have choices about their own abilities to connect with others and communicate well. We believe it is this ability to choose that creates the context for your actions and plans, allows you to commit to what you believe in, and gives you the capacity to learn and grow.

If individuals can understand what drives their choices, interactions, and reactions, they can use that insight to get to the root of who they are, what is truly important to them, and how they can then influence their worlds. Even when they believe they have no command or influence on what is going on around them, they do. In fact, it is when individuals affect and alter their own personal actions and reactions, that they do have some level of power in any situation.

What no one has, however, is the power to control the world. Life is too complex—there are too many

layers of overlapping events, triggered by multiple and varied causes, and governed by forces beyond their ken. In fact, control in such a convoluted, interdependent, and massively entangled world is, in fact, impossible.

While many people are relatively successful in navigating the paths they set, they most often do it by trial and error. They think something might work, so they try it. Then if it doesn't work, they try something else. If it does work, they remember and try it as an approach in subsequent challenges. The problem is that they cannot build any reliability that way. When things work and when they don't work, people cannot know why. Their explanations can only, at best, be an educated guess.

Even though people cannot control the world, they can, in fact, influence the multiple and entangled patterns of their lives. This book offers one approach to help individuals influence the dynamics that swirl about them.

Inquiry

The field of human systems dynamics (HSD) provides a collection of concepts and tools to see, understand, and influence patterns. Using simple metaphors adopted from nature, you can better grasp what is happening in your everyday interactions. *Simple Rules* is one of those metaphors that comes from the science of complex systems—like your own life. We believe HSD offers powerful tools for feeding the signal fires of your own journey.

Another critical tool we borrowed from HSD is the concept of inquiry and its role in understanding and influencing patterns in complex systems. Inquiry is the act of asking questions and believing the answer is not already known. To stand in inquiry is to go past what you think you know and to seek authentic answers. It is to allow yourself to be wrong, to be surprised, to see the world in new ways. Living in inquiry is to live in the questions that help you understand your life and your world.

> *"There are no good answers. The world changes too quickly. What works for you in this space and time may or may not work for me. There are only good questions. I can best understand and influence the patterns in life when I ask about the nature of those patterns and then test those assumptions in my own life."*
>
> ~Glenda Eoyang

This book is written to share our inquiry and expand on our own questions about the role simple rules can play in creating our own paths. It is our confidence in the wisdom, language, and simplicity of these HSD methods and tools that drives our own shared and individual inquiries into who we are and how we engage with the world.

We call this process radical because it asks powerful questions about our lives. We share Radical Inquiry here because engaging in the process invites you to stand in a place of questioning and not-knowing as you explore the very roots of who you are and what you are about. We hope to ignite your enthusiasm for this radical quest and support you through a powerful process of self-exploration and development.

> **Radical**: relating to or affecting the foundational nature of a thing.
>
> **Radical Inquiry** invites you to ask questions about your own foundational nature.

This book and our own experiences, as we share them here, stand as both the underpinning and cheerleading for your efforts. As people get clearer and more articulate about who they are and what they want in the world, they are in a better position to encourage others around them to do the same. We are lifelong learners at heart and support the idea that what people do to inquire into their own lives sustains and enhances growth and development for everyone.

Our agenda in writing this book is to present exciting, powerful ideas. Everyone has a story, and we offer this process as a way to help you identify and/or clarify yours. More importantly, we have found an even greater depth in these tools. If you find your story is no longer true or useful to you or that is does not serve you well, these tools can help you write a new chapter.

Be forewarned: There may be unintended consequences ahead. Your life may change through the examination and reconsideration of your own simple rules. This process may shift how you relate to the people in your life. It may increase the level of confidence and competence with which you greet each and every day.

You may find your own sense of self expanded and reinforced in how you view the world and your place in it.

That is the power that's possible in engaging in Radical Inquiry. Don't worry. Even though this is an engaging process that can be life changing, it is also a process that is simple and takes you at your own speed. You don't need any complicated tools or specialized skills. You don't have to be afraid that you'll be asked to do anything you cannot do. All you need is the commitment to sit with your questions and listen with an open heart and mind to the answers that lie within you. Rest assured: you CAN do it!

Seeking Fitness

Remember a time not too long ago when your life was uncomplicated and carefree? Summer lasted forever. Your world was focused on you and those people around you. You knew who your best friend was. And every decision you made affected only you.

Life is just not that way any more. Now there is your significant other. Or perhaps there are just others who have become significant to you. Then there is the baby on the way, parents growing older, that stack of bills to pay, or friends who need your help. There is your commitment at the shelter or the block party to plan—not to mention your job. Then there are hobbies … Poetry? Origami? Dog grooming? … Well, you get it. That is your story—your life today.

Something in you drew you to pick up this book. Something in you is looking for a new signal fire. We are not here to judge or change your life for you. We offer a way you can reframe your life so its purpose and meaning remain true to what you want, sustaining your growth and development, even as you attend to the life you have built.

Our premise is that simple rules help you make choices about how you participate in your life—day-to-day and minute-by-minute. They provide the means by which you can influence and shift your actions and the patterns in your life toward fitness. Now many people think about fitness as having physical strength and endurance to run a marathon. Our definition of fitness means the degree to which we fit in our worlds. It is a measure of physical and emotional health, social well-being and functioning, and all-around satisfaction. For example, fitness describes how you get along in your immediate environment and how well you continue to grow and develop. That is the measure of your fitness.

People are most fit when they are thoughtful in their habits, and their choices move them toward the next signal fire. This means your choices comprise the very meticulous practice of consciously maintaining fitness so it becomes part of you.

The inquiry that stokes your signal fires focuses on three questions.

- **Who are you?** What is your identity and what does that mean day-to-day?

- **What is important to you?** What is your motivation? What do you value?

- **How do you connect with others?** How do you relate with those around you and the world at large?

Join us in this place of inquiry. Open yourself to exploring something different, in a new and radical way, about YOU. Question, seek, decide, push, pull, poke, prod—examine what you think and know—and what you think you know—to find a new perspective about you and how you fit in your life. Get to the root of you.

What truly makes this process a work of Radical Inquiry is that you dig deep into yourself, down to the roots. Standing in the space of your questions, the ideas that spur you on light the next signal fire that draws you forward. Recognize just how drastic this is: The questions you ask will be far more important than the answers! And tomorrow's questions flow from today's responses.

When you stand in a place of inquiry, everything around you becomes potential data and a source of growth and development. You depart from the usual or customary; and you seek to change your life one radical piece at a time.

Our Assumptions

This book is based on our assumptions about this work, and our assumptions are grounded in the theory and practice of HSD. Before we begin, we want to share these assumptions with you because we know and appreciate that not everyone thinks the same things and in the same way. Unless you know where we stand, some of this work may not make sense to you. Our basic assumptions about this work frame our approach.

I.   We live and learn in a soup of complexity, unpredictability, surprise, and disquiet. Humans, as individuals or groups, have complex relationships, interactions, and experiences. Think of all the people we know, the places we go, the words we speak and the feelings we share. They are all massively entangled with each other. What we do in one place and/or time can change not just our own experience of the world, but can alter others' lives in ways we cannot predict. This does not mean life cannot also be joyful, engaging, challenging, and fulfilling. Our lives are what we make them, and if we understand the patterns around us, we are better able to influence our patterns toward fitness and growth.

II.   Patterns are the pieces of the puzzle that we are, individually and together. To learn what our motivations are, we have only to look at and understand the patterns of behavior and interaction that characterize our lives. Going way down deep and figuring out what matters to us and how important it really is takes energy and commitment. Getting to the root of who we are as individuals is what makes this inquiry difficult and radical.

III. What makes it different from any other self-help process is that this is such a radical approach, and we can do it ourselves—in fact we must do it ourselves. This book can guide us; a personal coach can be a sounding board; others can cheerlead from the sidelines. But we must be willing to come to a place of understanding and be patient enough to proceed at our own pace.

IV. Changing patterns is a thoughtful—and thought-provoking—business. When we make choices, we slow down, consider carefully, and learn to pay attention to the ways we currently behave, think, act, and learn. Those are our current patterns. If we want to change, we focus on identifying patterns that might be more effective. We consider actions and attitudes that encourage those patterns. We plan to create those conditions intentionally. It's not a one-time proposition. It is, in fact, a continuous reflection about where we are, where we want to be, and how we can best get there.

Sometimes it is as simple and straightforward as saying yes instead of saying no; as taking a deep breath and letting someone else answer first; as asking ourselves "Why?" or "Why not?" each time before we take an impulsive step. Instead of following current patterns without thinking, we step back and ask what is going on, think about what we want to do about it, and clarify why that is the action that will move us most effectively toward our goals. Perhaps we just need to calm down, count to 100, and make a different choice. Even a simple adjustment can break an old cycle and allow for new opportunities and options.

The point here is that it is all about taking time to consider and formulate the response that will move us toward fitness and growth.

Slow and steady wins the inquiry race. Slowing down also gives us time to engage in deep inquiry. When we take time for this type of inquiry into who we are, we create enough space to reinforce our intentions over time. Behaviors become thoughtful habits.

Dedicating time and energy to get to know ourselves is a significant piece of the process. What are our hot buttons? What cools us down? What are the implications of doing something different? What will be the result of paying attention to how we impact others? These and other questions will deepen our inquiry, and when we slow down and pay attention, the answers will come. At first it may seem awkward and false. Once we get into this thoughtful habit, however, the process will make sense and flow naturally.

You really can do it!

Conclusion

Here is our plan for moving with you into this new territory.

Chapter 2 provides the foundations of this work. We introduce you to and examine the nature and variety of systems and how they populate the world. We continue with a discussion of patterns, how they form, and how they influence our lives.

Chapter 3 further explores the nature of simple rules. We review what they are, examine how they are created, and discover how we can make them work for us. This chapter also describes the nature of a Radical Inquiry.

Chapter 4 presents two powerful tools for your own Radical Inquiry. The first is the Adaptive Action Cycle, a process that forces you to slow down and engage in more intentional and productive decision making and planning. The second tool is the Legacy Sustainability Model, designed to help you think about how parts of your world are connected. It helps build your own capacity to sustain new patterns that emerge from your Radical Inquiry.

Chapter 5 offers a way for you to recognize how these concepts come alive for you every day. Using simple examples this chapter walks you through the steps of a Radical Inquiry into Adaptive Action Planning. You will see how these processes can shape your thinking and behavior.

Chapter 6 shares our story. It provides an inside view of our own journey of using this process of exploring, identifying, and developing our simple rules. This chapter will take you through our thinking as we were writing this book and provide a vivid illustration of what we mean by both the simplicity and the complexity of simple rules.

Chapter 7 provides additional tools to help you plan how you will begin to implement your simple rules and shift your own patterns. These tools will deepen your understanding of how to apply these processes in a variety of settings.

Chapter 8 is a call to action. *Simple Rules* is about doing, and we offer a glimpse of what is, what can be, and what's next for all who want to engage in the ongoing path of lifelong Radical Inquiry. We offer you an opportunity to become One In A Million (OIAM) and create a sustainable world.

It is our intention that these eight chapters serve as a series of signal fires for you. The first purpose of our fires is to mark a path to understanding the underlying dynamics of relationships and connections inside the system that is you. The next is to offer you a mirror to help you understand the patterns in your life, what they mean, where they come from, and how they impact your everyday journey. The third purpose of these signal fires is to help you define your process to create change—to recognize your stories, shift your patterns, choose to move forward to a more coherent life path—to find greater fitness in your world.

Our signal fires are the ways in which we connect with you on a new and meaningful path. We encourage you to do something different, to trigger a shift in your system, alter your patterns, change your world view, and create a new impact on yourself and the people in your life.

Go ahead and turn the page: Grand possibilities await!

CHAPTER 2

Imagine it's 4 p.m. and you're traveling home in your car on Interstate 5 in San Diego, California. If you've ever actually been there, you may either smile or grimace at the memory. Cars move in an orchestrated dance, reflecting the ebb and flow of traffic patterns. You know these steps and stops, leaps and lurches. You track patterns, knowing if you leave home by 6:10 am, you'll be at your desk by 7:00. If, on the other hand, you miss that window, it'll take over 90 minutes for the same trip.

As you move along, suddenly, a line of red taillights appears. Traffic stops. Whatever has *happened – probably a fender bender – you wait for the stream of vehicles to adjust and start moving again. Even though the mishap responsible for the shift the action has nothing to do with you, you are influenced by actions and reactions of others. You could exit at the next right and find your way home, or you could stay where you are and see what happens. Which option makes the most sense to you right now?*

Your decision is based on available data: what you know to be true, updates on the radio, and whatever circumstances await you at home. You decide to stay on the road and call ahead. You find that dinner can wait but your son's study group has to be at the library on time. So you will have to pick the kids up instead of dropping them off, if your neighbor hasn't already left for her board meeting. You call her, and she hasn't left and says she is happy to trade if you will also pick up her older daughter, Lynn, at her job. This extra stop means you will have to record the second half of the basketball game and watch it tomorrow. That's fine, as long as no one tells you the score in the morning before you have a chance to watch the game.

No problem. This is just the way systems work.

In this chapter, we move from systems theory grounded in human systems dynamics to practice and common examples illustrating how this knowledge and your own influence can transform action and results.

Welcome to Systems

So, what exactly is a system? It is a collection of individuals or parts that interrelate with, and mutually depend on, one another to function as a working

whole. That's the formal definition; now let's talk about what that means to you.

Your family is a system that operates in the larger context of the neighborhood where you live. As you drive home you participate and contribute to the system of traffic movement on the interstate. Your children are a part of the system that is their school, drawing you in as you interact with their teachers and attend their sporting and performance events. Each of these smaller subsystems is a part of a greater system that is the community or city. The parts are interactive and interdependent on each other, responding to what happens in the whole.

In addition to the system of commuters that lengthened your trip home and the neighborhood support system adjusted according to your needs, other examples of systems include the human body; families, teams, and organizations; global markets; faith communities; and your local fire department. The parts of a system are linked together. The links may be physical (the hip bone is connected to the thigh bone), functional (agency volunteers communicate with their work staff), or relational (you and Suzi have been best friends since 3rd grade).

You, yourself, are part of myriad systems in both your personal and professional lives. This includes everything from your mahjong league to the homeowners' association, your political party to your collective bargaining unit.

Another way to think about systems is to reflect on how the parts of a system relate to each other. Think about your family's Thursday night schedule—people are coming and going, and dinner gets prepared and eaten somehow. Eventually everyone gets home to bed. Consider the regular post-game repartee regarding local team rivalries at work; and the easy give and take that makes good neighbors. Or, imagine a fender bender during rush hour in the High Occupancy Vehicle lane on the way to work.

The parts of a system function interdependently toward a common purpose or particular outcome, and the combination of these parts gives the system properties or qualities not found in any of the separate pieces alone. Think of a group or team that accomplishes more together than the members could if they worked independently. The ways they contribute to each other's work enriches the final product and makes it possible to do more.

Systems can be small, with only a few components, or larger, with more interacting parts that are all linked. The simplest social systems could be a few people governed by a limited number of rules or customs, such as a carpool. This carpool does not, however, function alone in the universe. Even with the small number of direct participants in the carpool, each person is still subject to influences from other parts of the greater system and bring multiple challenges to this smaller system—this week's driver overslept and made everyone else late; one person called in sick today, and the trip is shorter because that stop is eliminated; one person's aging parents cause her consternation that makes her distracted and irritable.

Larger complex social systems include many more people and more diverse rules and customs. This could be an entire company, state agency, or faith community. Customs here would include celebration of rituals, appropriate dress for congregants, and observing dietary laws.

Just so you know, larger systems do not necessarily mean greater complexity. Think about the relationship between a child's local school, the larger city or area school system, and even larger national or regional education systems. Each is separate yet connected, independent and at the same time

interdependent, having its own dependencies, interactions, and complexities.

All social systems are open to outside influences. A public school in the United States, for example, though it functions within four brick walls, is open to outside influences such as a blizzard, which creates a snow day; a tricky union negotiation, which may close the cafeteria; or a presidential election, which turns the building into a polling place. The election cycles actually create—in that same elementary school's space—a different human social system that emerges, expands, culminates, contracts and then begins to build again in its own four-year cycle.

A social system may also emphasize flexibility, countless communication paths, and collaboration. They have boundaries that may be more or less clearly delineated, and parts of one system may flow across those boundaries into other parts of the system. These systems are neither predictable nor controllable.

Think about a family reunion. Who attends? Who speaks to whom? Who always tells an offensive joke? When these kinds of things happen, an open system responds. People find each other; those who are not speaking aren't put at the same table; and someone always apologizes for the bad joke.

When something in a complex system goes wrong, parts of the system respond and adapt. Don't even bother to look for a root cause. Every event is generated by a previous event and influenced by multiple factors in the system.

Human systems are actually systems within systems, connected to other systems. For instance you, as an individual, are an open system made up of bodily systems that maintain your health.

Your physical systems—circulatory, digestive, respiratory, nervous, integumentary, and reproductive —all help your body stay alive by taking in nourishment and by responding to the environment. At the same time, you, as an individual system, are part of greater systems—family, work group, faith community, neighborhood, or political parties. At times, the parts seem to reside in each other like nested dolls, with what seems like very little connection. As an entity, a family can function relatively independently from the political party to which the parents belong.

At other times, systems appear to be massively entangled due to their relationships and connections. For example, a family might be actively involved in neighborhood activities: little brother is on the local baseball team, sister has just started going steady with the boy next door, mom has organized a car pool for her work colleagues who live in the area, and dad heads up the annual neighborhood garage sale.

An elementary school is an open system, and so are the teachers' association, the math club, and the school newspaper. From another angle, school teachers all report to their school principal; school principals report to their district superintendent; and the district superintendent reports to the school board.

Their interconnectedness and multiple similarities and differences all relate to the nature of systems. What happens in one part of the system affects the whole; what happens to the whole affects the parts, and it all happens in ways that can neither be predicted nor controlled, no matter how you try.

The open exchange of information and responses between and among the parts of a system allows for alterations and modifications within the system that then trigger other responses and modifications. This is the nature of the adaptability that characterizes these systems.

Think about the scenario that introduced this chapter. During that ride home you can sit in your car and wait out the traffic jam, get off the Interstate at a different exit than usual and take the back roads home, or decide upon a third, fourth, or fifth alternative.

Changing your response at any point along the way will shift your impact on the system in unpredictable and uncontrollable ways. You get home in time take your son to the library, so you don't have to pick up the neighbor's daughter. Also you don't have to record the ball game and can talk about it with your buddies in the morning.

Complex or Complicated?

No, they are not the same, although they are often used interchangeably.

Complex means something is composed of many interdependent parts and is inherently unpredictable. A complex system has rules you can learn, but you can neither predict nor control how the parts interact in any specific situation or at any specific time. Changing or interfering with one part of a complex system can cause unexpected consequences in other parts that may seem distant and removed. Finally when you take apart a complex system, the parts alone cannot behave like the system itself, and it cannot be reconstructed again in just the same way. A complex system is more than the sum of its parts.

Complicated, on the other hand, comes from a Latin word that means "folded together." A complicated system is made up of individual parts that, when taken apart, are recognizable as independent parts. The whole is just the parts working together.

Complex Adaptive Systems

Human beings live and work in complex adaptive systems (CAS). *Complex* reflects the parts of the system and subsystems are connected in multiple ways, and they are mutually supporting and reliant. You cannot change one thing without having an impact on everything else—in either big ways or small.

The Butterfly Effect is a popular phenomenon that is used as an example of how things are connected in a CAS. It is a supposition made by a scientist who studied weather systems. Basically what it says is that if a butterfly flapped its wings on the coast of Asia, that such a small shift in the air—given all the right conditions—could cause a huge weather event on the coast of South America.

Even if you do not believe that a butterfly flapping its wings in Asia affects the weather several thousand miles away, you can think about the last time you were walking down a busy city street. Now, imagine that you turned left instead of right. How might you, your day, and the world have been different?

This question—enticing and titillating as it is—has been explored in books, movies, poetry, and song. The real reason it is so exciting is that in a complex system, we cannot know how any one change will impact the whole. It fires the imagination to consider infinite possibilities.

Adaptive expresses the capacity to change, react, or adjust in response to actions, behaviors, or conditions of the system's environment. As the parts of a system respond to changes in the environment or in each other, they shift conditions across the system. Each part of a system seeks fitness as it responds to shifts around it. In a complex system, the sole purpose

of adaptation is to seek fitness and contribute to sustainability.

Examples of adaptation in a complex system:

- It's happened to most everyone. When it rains on the day of the family reunion, everyone shifts to option B, moving into the shelter.
- When your preferred way of building relationships no longer works, you find other ways to connect to others.
- When we believe something is dangerous, we get that rush of adrenalin that fuels the *fight or flight* response.

These two human characteristics—*complexity* and *adaptability*—describe systems where individuals act in a variety of unpredictable and interconnected ways. These individuals themselves are "semiautonomous" in that, even though there are rules and expectations for their behavior and work, they are free to choose what to do next in the context of their surroundings.

That is why they are unpredictable, like the combined actions of all the members that form the phenomenon that is a family. It is unique and complex —unpredictable and uncontrollable. In general you can anticipate how people you know will respond, but at any given point in time you cannot really KNOW how they will respond to a particular event because you cannot know the multiple factors that will influence their responses. This is true of individuals. It is also true of groups, organizations, communities, or nations.

Systems and Self-Organization

To make sense of the world and work toward greater fit, a CAS will adjust (adapt) to the demands of its environment, responding to changes. This is a constant and continuous process of *self-organizing*. Simply put, self-organization is the ongoing work of the parts of a system as they do what it takes to help the system adjust to environmental influences. While *self* seems to imply that this is only about an individual, it actually applies to both the individual and the whole. *The system is the self*, whether it is a single individual, group, community, or nation.

For example, when a young person relocates for her first job, she is anxious, excited, and a bit disoriented. In response to her new circumstances, she begins to *self-organize*, finding a place to live and ways to navigate new roads and destinations. She starts the new job, begins to make friends, and discovers convenient local amenities, such as a library, the supermarket, and a doctor. Some of these goals are easier to achieve than others; some require flexibility and patience. Yet, slowly but surely she finds her bearings in these new conditions and purposefully develops processes and expectations to manage the functions of her new routine.

Or, let us return to the traffic stand-still on Interstate 5. Unfortunately this kind of thing happens time and again, so fortunately you are prepared. You carry a set of books or CDs you can listen to; you ask *Martha*, your GPS, to find you an alternate route home; or you decide to get off at the next exit and pop in to see that foreign film that no one else you know is interested in. You have learned that honking your horn or shouting at the car in front of you has little or no impact on the situation, except that it irritates others and frustrates you. You know this because you have tried this approach, and it does not work.

Also, changing lanes, as a few feet between cars opens up, is counterproductive. It winds up taking longer, and other drivers are less considerate of this behavior. Go on, pop a CD into your player and hear

the new best-selling thriller read to you by James Earl Jones in that wonderful, rich honey-like voice that soothes your nerves and captures your imagination.

The sum of these thoughts and actions is *you* self-organizing in response to unexpected changes in your system. That is how individuals "organize" themselves to work together, and move toward shared goals, whether they are stated or not. A family's shared goal is to be a family: it is quite practical and logical for each member to recognize individual and collective needs as they settle into a new community, make friends, and enjoy what they come to value in a newly emerging family life. Individuals self-organize to meet their own goals; groups, communities, and organizations self-organize toward shared goals.

It is critical to remember that self-organization is a continuous process. Self-organization happens whether we are looking or not—whether we are paying attention or not. It is automatic—we don't choose to or choose not to self-organize. We respond to changes in our world—even if it's just to notice a change and decide not to take any action. The decision not to act is, in itself, a response.

Self-organization is active: choosing, adapting, and then potentially thriving. It creates the patterns of interaction and behavior that come to characterize our lives.

Patterns: Similarities, Differences, and Relationships

Patterns of interaction and behavior in your life come from how you act, react, think, and respond to form the cohesive whole that you are; the cohesive whole that becomes a personality; the cohesive whole that becomes a life. In Human Systems Dynamics

(HSD), *patterns* are defined as similarities, differences, and relationships that have meaning over space and time.

Across the many systems where you operate, you come to know people by their patterns. You define people by their characteristic actions or traits. When people are kind and generous in all areas of their life, you describe them that way. In the same way, you come to know groups by the characteristics that separate you from them—different social customs, different religious beliefs and practices, different histories—or by the characteristics that make them similar to you—common faith practices, cultural customs, shared histories. These patterns contribute to the richness of a diverse experience—or they are the patterns that are the seeds of bias and prejudice. It is about patterns of similarities, differences, and relationships that have come to have meaning over time.

People generally characterize group and individual patterns in polar terms. They talk of patterns of abundance or scarcity, optimism or despair, energetic activity or slow deliberation. The truth is that they generate multiple patterns in their lives, depending on their circumstances. Sometimes those patterns are more or less productive, more or less stable, more or less engaging. Patterns just are what they are, and they emerge from ongoing choices individuals and groups make about their behaviors and relationships as they self-organize in response to various situations.

Every time people act, they reinforce the patterns through their behavior, which, in turn, reinforces the behavior. When some people find themselves in new situations, they tend to maintain a low profile at first. They gather some data and assess their new space. Eventually they become accustomed to their new environments, beginning to feel more comfortable.

That is a common pattern: they get to know what's going on before they jump in; they feel safer and more confident; they come to trust their instincts. Success reinforces their behavior.

Other people get their reinforcement by jumping right in and figuring it out by trial and error. When they feel successful with that strategy, they try it again and again.

Sometimes individuals outgrow patterns that may have worked in the past but cease to serve them well over time. They abandon these patterns and experiment with new approaches until they find patterns that work for them again.

The same phenomenon is true in families, groups, and organizations. People begin to interact with each other in ways that are productive and helpful. They begin to establish behavior patterns and expectations that fit their needs.

New patterns emerge, and begin to influence current behavior, requiring more people to conform to those expectations and fit into the prevailing patterns of behavior. This compliance with expectations and existing patterns reinforces the overriding patterns.

> "Nina and I have been good friends since college days. Though the times we see each other are few and far between, when we do get together, our conversation picks up where we last left off. We do not miss a beat from one meeting to the next, we have a pattern of continuous and enjoyable engagement across the years and miles."
>
> ~Mallary

This cyclic dynamic of behaviors generating patterns that, in turn, reinforce behaviors is often evident in communities or organizations. We refer to it as *culture*. Culture is the culmination of dominant patterns of behavior that characterize a group; a reinforcing template shaping what we do and how we think. Different types of patterns create different types of cultures in different places.

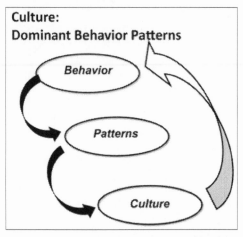

Early in the development of the United States, a culture developed that favored white men who owned land or found other ways to be economically stable. Those white men of money and power came together and created laws that protected that privilege; they elected representatives who maintained that status for them, and they established schools and universities that educated their sons to step into that role as they came of age. This pattern of privilege ignored women, people of color, and any individual who was not financially fit.

Over the past 100 years, that culture has changed. Women and minorities were granted the right to vote. Poll taxes were repealed. The civil rights movement of the 1960s and the women's liberation movement of 1970s shined a light on a culture made up of patterns

of inequality and bias. New patterns emerged that allowed for previously marginalized individuals and groups to have a voice in their workplaces, communities, and voting booths. While many patterns have shifted, some old behaviors and expectations remain under scrutiny as the system that is the United States continues to change.

Because we make up these complex adaptive systems, once we become aware of patterns we do not like or want, we can do something about it. We make a conscious choice to change our behavior. New behaviors lead to new patterns; new patterns create a new culture; and the emerging new culture supports different behaviors across the system.

In every moment *WE* have the power to influence the system and how it self-organizes. We cannot control what happens, but we can take specific steps to intervene or interrupt current patterns. We choose our behaviors based on what is important to us and what we believe. Not only can we influence what is going on around us; we can choose to do so or not.

Setting the Conditions for Change

Within complex adaptive systems, three conditions shape the patterns that emerge. Glenda Eoyang has identified these three conditions through her work, human systems dynamics. As we gain more understanding about these conditions, our ability to influence them and alter the patterns in our lives grows.

The first condition is the *container,* which sets boundaries, binds the system, and holds it together. The container may be physical, such as an office or the human body. Containers can be social, such as a family unit or a congregation. Containers can also be psychological. Identity, anger, and affinities are examples of psychological containers.

In the example about development of culture in the United States, the containers were first aligned according to gender, race, and economic status. Social containers helped to maintain the divisions as rich white families married their children to each other, perpetuating those strong boundaries.

Groups were marginalized according to the containers that defined them. Women had their roles, people of color had their positions in the larger container, and poor people "knew their place." It was only through the powerful actions of some very brave individuals that these containers began to shift, and new containers began to emerge.

The second condition is ***difference***. Differences provide the potential for interaction and change within a system. In human systems, differences and distinctions, such as power, gender and affiliation generate activity, movement, and energy. In a CAS, the strongest patterns emerge around the differences that are believed to have the greatest impact on the system.

In the early days of the United States, founders believed that differences around gender, finances, and color were what determined their own abilities to lead. The movements to ensure civil rights for all citizens were all about saying that traditional differences of gender, race, or economic status were not differences that mattered. The culture generated by these movements is one where other differences— commitment and skill, for instance—are what matter.

The third condition is ***exchanges***, or the flow and movement of information or resources, between and among members of the system. Exchanges can include meetings, gestures, data, feedback, money, and rules. The quality of any exchange lies in its effectiveness in bringing about change and facilitating adaptation and self-organization that generates new patterns.

The power of activists like Martin Luther King, Jr. and Betty Friedan; the actions of small groups of committed individuals like Rosa Parks; and the shifting social norms of post World War II in the United States—all of these are examples of exchanges that contributed to significant system changes in the American culture in the later part of the 20th Century.

These three primary conditions—containers, differences, and exchanges—exist in every complex adaptive system, and it is the interplay between and among them that determines patterns and system-wide culture. In fact, because they are so entangled and interdependent, even a slight shift in one will influence and lead to shifts in others.

As you sit in meetings at your work or participate in social gatherings in your community, you are part of complex systems—and you bring with you multiple containers, differences, and exchanges. You belong in the container we call *women* or *men;* you may be known by the religious or faith container with which you identify; you may be known by the work you do, the friends you have, or the hobbies you pursue. At the same time, in that or any container there are multiple ways you are similar to or different from others. Even when you are in the container marked Woman, your role is different from other women— even doing the same job in the same company—as are the expectations and ways you communicate with others. If you changed any one of these, however, that could trigger changes across them all.

By understanding and paying attention to these dynamics, you have the power to influence the system significantly, changing how it organizes, and potentially shifting its outcomes. You can have an impact on the direction you go, how fast you get there, and why it is so critical to make the attempt.

Conditions for our own self-organization are easy to discern and can be distilled down to three simple questions.

- Who am I? *(The Container)*
- What is important to me? *(The Difference)*
- How do I want to/ How do I connect with others? *(The Exchanges)*

Your own patterns emerge from your behaviors. The Radical Inquiry we describe in this book is a process of deeply examining and understanding the patterns that characterize your life and the ways in which you pursue your dreams. We will be inviting you to dive into the deep end of the pool through your Radical Inquiry, seeing and understanding those patterns that characterize your life, and looking for more adaptive and productive patterns. At its heart, the Radical Inquiry process is about engaging in these questions.

- What actions are in my own best interest?
- Are they consistent with who I am?
- Are they consistent with what I believe?
- Are they consistent with how I relate to those around me?

Once you have defined the patterns you want in your life, you can then begin to create your simple rules to generate those patterns. This whole process is designed to get to the root of your *self*—how you are in the world, what is important to you, what motivates you, what keeps your focus and attention; what leads your exploration, and what guides your relationships with others and the world.

As we think about the cultural forces at work today, in the 21st Century, we see changing and emergent patterns. Technology is altering how we each communicate, process, and manage information. Telecommunications, advances in transportation, and high levels of mobility are changing the ways we think about connecting with community, friendships, and family. Baby boomers and Generation X-ers work every day, side by side in shared containers we call organizations. Global economies and environmental priorities bring us together, while political and social polarization tears us apart. All of these shifting, worldwide patterns call on us to understand what is happening and do what we can to influence the world toward sustainability.

Conclusion

In this chapter, we explored the concept of a complex adaptive system, applying the concepts of patterns and adaptations in our own lives. We talked about our own abilities to understand and shift the conditions of self-organization to bring about change in our lives.

We believe that at the heart of this work lies a short list of simple rules. The simple rules are your foundation. They guide your decisions, actions, and responses in ways that help you shift the conditions to create patterns of health and productivity. By engaging in an internal dialogue of inquiry and intention, you can bring about the changes you want to see. It is time to begin that dialogue with yourself.

Chart your course and weigh anchor. The journey awaits you. There is the next signal fire, up ahead.

CHAPTER 3

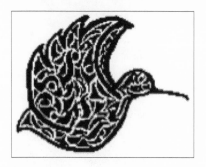

Simple rules are like the DNA of human behavior and decision making. They carry the code of our values and beliefs, informing our every move. Whether we are aware of them or not, they are there, helping us make choices in the moment and across time.

In the Introduction we named the concepts we believe are the foundation for the work we invite you to do in a Radical Inquiry. We started with a general description of the concept of simple rules to help you see the deepest dynamics of this work. In Chapter 2 we shared ideas about systems, self-organizing, and the notion and nature of patterns, which are shaped by behaviors, interactions, and choices in all areas of life.

Now in Chapter 3, we bring the two pieces together to show how your simple rules lie at the heart of your behaviors and patterns. In this chapter we will continue to build on this learning to help you establish your own foundation for a Radical Inquiry. Stay with us on this journey—take advantage of those unexpected responses, events, places, and consequences that wait for you.

Simple Rules: Where? What? Why? How?

Few of us are aware of simple rules and their role in our interactions and behaviors. Even some scientists and theorists who have studied complex adaptive systems in great detail remain skeptical and don't agree that simple rules even exist. For now, however, we are asking you to suspend your judgments and come with us on this journey to talk how the idea of simple rules offers each of us a bit of hope. We believe they are key to your clarity about what's important and how you want to relate to others in your world; they are also key to bringing about significant change in your life.

Simple rules are one example of the signal fires you watch for and signal fires you light for others. They are critical to your self-organizing—toward a brighter tomorrow and the swell of *self-hope* in your own life.

The Origin of Simple Rules

Simple rules have emerged from the thinking of technicians and researchers who use computer simulations to study the behavior of phenomena in their environments. These theorists have studied how birds flock in the beautiful and graceful ways they do; they study shifting patterns of urban growth; how populations of animals change in the wild; and many other complex ideas and concepts. What they discovered is that if they give a computer very simple rules about how something behaves, they can set the computer in motion and it will generate patterns on the screen that represent fairly accurately what they see in nature.

For example, using as few as three rules, a computer simulation can create intricate and elegant patterns that look like birds flocking. Those rules are:

• Steer toward the average position of local flock mates.

• Match the average speed of the flock.

• Steer to avoid crowding.

In other words ...

• Fly toward the center of the flock.

• Fly at the same general speed as everybody else.

• Don't fly into anyone.

You can go online and do a search for *BOIDS* or *Craig Reynolds* to find sites where you can make up your own rules and see what happens on the screen. Notice how patterns change with slight alterations in the rules. A small change in one rule can have a big change in the overall simulated flock pattern. Imagine then how changing your own simple rules can help you shift your patterns of behavior.

We have taken the idea of simple rules from computer simulations and have applied it to human behavior and interaction. We recognize this as a metaphor, and we know that birds probably don't actually keep repeating those three rules over and over to themselves as they fly south for the winter. Nor do we believe that the lovely sound of geese honking as they fly through the clouds is actually their way of yelling at each other about whether or not they are obeying the simple rules.

We do, however, believe that this metaphor is a useful means to help you think about changing your life. We also believe that with rigor and consistency in developing and applying your own simple rules, you can identify and create the patterns you wish to see in your life.

That is what this book is about, and we are asking you to take a leap of faith with us. Follow along and see where this path takes you.

What Simple Rules Do for Us

As we stated in Chapter 2, we suggest that every individual has a set of simple rules that governs behavior on a day-to-day basis, and those behaviors, over time, create patterns that characterize who they are and what they are about. Think about what is central and foundational in your family. Is this accidental or is this deliberate?

We also suggest that groups of individuals who work and live together over time create an underlying set of simple rules that establish patterns of interaction and thought. This is true even if the members of a family or office don't intentionally articulate those rules. Beyond mission statements and the corporate vision, think about the basics of what is important at work and how your team functions and relates to each other. Is this random or is this intentional?

If you articulate your list of simple rules, they can help you know, at any given moment, how you should behave, relevant to what is important. You encounter thousands of questions and exchanges in an ordinary day, and at each point, you make a decision. That decision may be as simple as which shoes you are going to wear, or it may be more complex, such as considering relationships and interactions with a widely diverse group of people.

Simple rules are at one and the same time the essence and result of your decision making. They provide a short-hand way of helping you make sure your decisions (and subsequent actions) are consistent with who you are, what you want, and how you want to *be* in the world. They also help you think about your decisions across time. If you have one set of rules that tells you how to respond and what is important, then you don't have to stop and think about what to do when a new person or a new situation presents itself. You already have a strategy for your actions.

This is what accounts for your behavior being consistent and somewhat predictable from day to day. It is important because this sense of predictability is what people come to count on in your relationships. It makes people feel safe to be around you; it's what makes you familiar. This is also what makes your simple rules so exquisitely personal: It is all about YOU.

Now, pause for a moment and think about some of the ways people would say you are predictable and familiar. Think about the elements of your decision-making process that might contribute to those more general behaviors.

• Your general worldview

• The rules you generally choose to obey

- The myriad factors in your environment that you pay attention to in general

Simple Rules Work in Groups

Remember that earlier we talked about how, without really thinking about it, individuals who live, work, or play together over a period of time create and maintain agreements that govern their behavior with each other—they create group simple rules. It is not likely a group's simple rules will be identical to those of the individual members. The group simple rules emerge from the ways the group members behave and interact, so it makes sense they will reflect the values of the individuals. The fact that individuals choose to participate in and maintain their membership in a particular group, supports the notion that, as members, they have come to an agreement to use those particular rules. Most often these agreements are implicit—people either stay and play by the rules or they leave. Sometimes a group will take the time to articulate the rules and engage each other explicitly to state and agree to use a set of simple rules.

Think about when you were growing up. There were probably rules or expectations that everyone knew and understood. *Dad (or Mom) is always right.* Or *Watch out for strangers.*

Or how about the shared agreement, "Call if you are going to be late." It's easy to understand how a simple phone call can alleviate stress or concern for family members who are waiting up when someone is late.

Simple rules even work for larger groups and communities. For instance, the Golden Rule is an example of a simple rule. "Do unto others as you would have them do unto you." has become, over time, a common principle that some people use to make decisions about their behavior. The tenets of any faith community also generally operate as a list of simple rules: from The Ten Commandments to the core ideas in the teachings of Buddha or the Koran.

As simple rules create consistency across the decisions in your life, you will establish patterns that characterize you as an individual, and others will begin to respond to you according to those predictable patterns. For example, if you use the Golden Rule to guide decisions and actions, then people will come to expect fair treatment and respect from you. Most people will, in turn, respond according to those expectations. The positive feedback and support will then reinforce further Golden-Rule behavior. If this cycle serves to get you what you want, the simple rule will become an even stronger force in your decision making.

Simple rules aren't always about being good and kind—they are about behaviors and patterns, and being intentional about what is desired. Surely you know someone who seemed to live by the simple rule, *Win at all costs*. Anyone with this simple rule would take advantage of others, creating questionable situations. These behaviors then would likely trigger further competitiveness and power brokering. It is a cycle that is hard to break—particularly since it seems to get the person what he or she wanted—to win.

Of course this example uses an extreme situation to make a point.

Still, think of the last time you tried to make a significant change in your life. From changing something about your personality to losing weight to managing money differently to experiencing a religious conversion—each of these desires for new or different outcomes calls for significant change that shifts the simple rules by which you interact with the world.

How Simple Rules Work

Simple rules guide behavior in consistent ways. As you respond and make decisions in the world, you need guidance knowing what actions and responses will help you get what you want—what you need to survive. You also need the predictability and consistency that simple rules help establish.

Simple rules provide that important guide. They are easy to remember. You should not have more than 5–7 simple rules because you would not be able to remember any more than that. They are broad statements that provide general direction, rather than just narrow, specific instructions. Additionally these broad statements should be applicable in an infinite number of situations.

Simple rules are generalizable—they guide you in almost any area of your life, no matter the context. There are wide-ranging rules that tell you what to do about specific events or decisions, but they may or may not be simple rules. If a rule tells you what to do in a specific situation, it's more of an instruction than a simple rule.

For instance, "Look both ways before crossing the street," is an instruction about how to get safely to the other side of the street. On the other hand it could be used as a metaphor to help you think about checking out all options, dangers, and opportunities that might be related to a particular decision or action. So as a simple rule, it could be useful in many areas and situations. If you don't mean it that broadly, it's not a simple rule.

Here are a couple of statements that are actually just instructions. But when they are used as metaphors, they can be generalized to a wide variety of situations.

- **Buy low; sell high.** In the stock market it means just what it says. To convert it to a simple rule, you have to think about how it might guide behavior in other situations. It could be generalized to mean that you always seek the best advantage, and you don't make a decision until you are sure you have.

- **Use only 140 characters.** Twitter, the online social networking media, limits messages to a maximum of 140 characters. That is an instruction. On the other hand, this statement could also be generalized to remind you to choose your words carefully or express yourself simply; don't share every thought; or don't overload others with too much information.

Remember when you are trying to create your simple rules, if you make a statement that would be applicable in only one or two situations, they are probably just instructions and not simple rules.

At the same time, any simple rules should be scalable, meaning that they can inform decisions at all levels, whether thinking about yourself, how to behave in relationships, or when you participate in larger groups in your life—family, community, work, or even the larger world beyond.

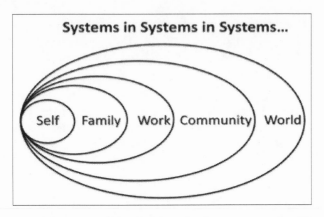

Systems in Systems in Systems...

Self) Family) Work) Community) World

Take a possible simple rule for an example: *Honor family*. As you will note, this rule is generalizable in that, whatever you do, you consider your impact on family. Each of your actions will then integrate and honor the concept of family.

Honor family is also scalable. *Scalable* means that your decisions are consistent, whether you are considering action at a personal level or at any level. Your simple rules guide your decisions about the community, your work, your nation, and even in your global perspective. Your decisions will align across all these scales.

For example, if your personal focus is on family, then when you make choices about your actions in the community, those choices also focus on families. Volunteering or charity work, community priorities you support, and commitments of time and energies, all come down on the side of family. At an even greater scale, you make decisions at the national or political level that will support families, as you define them. There may be people who don't agree with the choices you ultimately make, but you apply your simple rule according to your interpretation. You use it consistently across all areas and at all levels of your life.

Not everyone is going to agree about what are the best simple rules to guide behavior. In a world that's so diverse, it is inevitable that individuals will develop different rules to guide their lives. What can be surprising, however, is that two people can talk about the same simple rule, but on closer examination, they realize that they mean very different things. For instance, given one set of experiences and worldview, *Honor family* has a specific meaning that might be far different from someone with another set of experiences. That one simple rule may provide those two individuals very different guidance for behavior and decision making.

When people operate from differing simple rules, they often come into conflict without really understanding why. For example, given the simple rule, *Honor family*, it is crucial to know what that means to each individual. What does it mean to honor something? How do you define family? If you can articulate and explore your separate interpretations, you have taken a first step toward negotiating across the differences. This is another reason to articulate and understand your own simple rules.

Simple rules work because, once you have formed habits around them, you don't have to keep repeating them to yourself to remember to use them— just like birds are in the habit of flying together without running into each other. Simple rules become a part of individuals' automatic responses and formulate the habits of their actions. Remember, habits are patterns, too.

However, habits are hard to break. To change habits, you have to identify and eliminate or change the simple rule (or rules) that drive a particular response, and replace it (them) with another rule that will provide helpful guidance. Then you have to practice using the new rule until it becomes as ingrained as the earlier response.

The time to change or eliminate a simple rule is when:

- You're not getting what you want because of the rules you currently have, as in the case of the win-at-all costs person above, or you have decided that what you want has changed.

- You don't have one that works in your current life situation. Children probably would not consider it important to have a simple rule about honoring family. Someone who has raised a family, however, might feel compelled to add this simple rule.

- You want to intentionally change your life. This is another way of saying that goals, priorities, and desired outcomes have shifted. People finally quit smoking when they change their simple rules. Rather than using other ways of calming, the one simple rule of *Breathe* may be a reminder to stop and think about what is going on and how to respond.

On the surface, *Breathe* might seem to be an instruction. But when it serves as a metaphor for all of life, it says, *Slow down and relax and make the choice that will lengthen your life*. Some people might use *Slow down and smell the roses*. Someone else might say *Push pause* as a metaphor for the same thing. Using a simple rule that has meaning for you and is memorable is the key.

Simple Rules Are Important

You are a complex individual who moves toward what you want in life in a world that is unpredictable and constantly changing. You interact every day with other individuals who are also moving toward their goals in an unpredictable and constantly changing world. As you interact with others, you make decisions about how to survive and thrive in the world. You constantly adapt to the changes and challenges that face you every moment.

Think about a cartoon character that is standing against a wall while table tennis balls are thrown at them in random and unpredictable ways. Imagine all the gyrations and positions and evasive measures that character might go through to avoid getting hit by one of those balls. Now imagine that you are that character, and as the balls come at you, you leap and turn to avoid being hit, and you catch some, tossing them away or back where they came from, kicking them aside or putting them in your pockets as a resource for later action, sharing them with your neighbors to help them deal with challenges.

That's basically how everyone goes through life … they go through all kinds of motions and actions to adapt to whatever the world is throwing at them. And since they are not cartoon characters that can be bent and drawn in any shape, what they need is something that will tell them how to bend without breaking as they respond and adapt to this unpredictable world.

Simple rules help inform reactions and interactions as people respond. They help them remain true to what's important as they consider the myriad challenges, options, and opportunities that come along. They make choices in the moment, every moment as they play out their strategies to survive and thrive.

You have the power and ability not only to be reflective in every decision you make, but to realize that in every choice lies the chance to change who you are. In every choice lies the chance to move one step closer to being the person you want to be and to achieving what is important in your life. In each moment you choose to move toward or away from fitness.

Using Radical Inquiry

We believe in the power of simple rules to create the essence of your life. We have designed a process to help guide you through a careful and thorough exploration of the patterns in your life and the simple rules that inform your actions. We call this process Radical Inquiry.

While your first inclination, when faced with a problem, is to offer solutions and begin fixing, we want you to start by inquiring into the patterns that currently exist and examine if they are coherent, consistent, and work for you. This entire process is actually an inquiry you undertake to clarify and define who you are and what you want to become. It is an inquiry designed to help you examine simple rules that currently dictate your choices, identify those that are helpful and healthy, and change those that are not.

This inquiry poses questions that enable you to consider how your actions currently shape your life. It also asks how you can reshape and shift areas of your life where you want a richer, fuller, and more meaningful existence.

In this stance of inquiry, the questions rather than the answers serve to move you forward. Questions like:

- What matters most?
- What is important?
- How do you want to connect with others?
- What do you want to accomplish?
- What do you dream?
- What is your vision?

Radical inquiry will help you take your answers to those questions, establish simple rules for living

that life, and guide you in mapping out specific steps to bring about productive and healthy patterns.

This is not merely a conversation you have with yourself. This exploration digs down to the essence of who you are, and provides a path for examining and then shifting that essence if you want to and are ready and willing to invest the time and energy. And this is where Self-Hope comes in.

We are asking you to think about your faith, expectations, and desires. What is it you dream about creating and doing? What do you hope to accomplish, reach, and complete? Where do you believe your destiny and legacy lie? What do you want for your children and your community and your world? Where does the hope for yourself and others lie? That is what this book is about: understanding and achieving what you hope for yourself and others—self-hope.

Conclusion

Simple rules are a foundation to Radical Inquiry because they represent a fundamentally different approach to self-examination and personal growth. This process does not prescribe a way to be. Instead, it helps you identify what you want in your life, and then takes you through a series of activities and reflections to help you develop your own blueprint.

Our approach is radical because it offers you concrete steps and activities that can, if you are willing to do the work, move you from where you are today to a life that is more coherent with the life you want.

In the next chapters, you learn about the process and power of Radical Inquiry as you seek out the next signal fire.

CHAPTER 4

"Hominid and human evolution took place over millions and not billions of years, but with the emergence of language there was a further acceleration of time and the rate of change."
~William Irwin Thompson

In this early part of the 21st century, change just isn't what it used to be. Diversity in all areas of life is expanding exponentially. Every year we know more people; we hear more different languages; we see a broader world—even a larger universe. We have more choices in almost every arena of living; we have more and varied *sources of news and information. We can connect with individuals and groups we never even knew existed before. In short, the signal fires that inform our lives are growing in number, size, and direction.*

William Irwin Thompson talks about the emergence of language and how it accelerates change. In Chapter 3 we provided an in-depth orientation to simple rules, how they are created and how we can make them work for us. Continuing on our journey, Chapter 4 offers two additional exciting tools to provide you with language to accelerate your own personal change. They are the Adaptive Action Cycle and the Legacy Sustainability Model.

We Need Agile Tools

Think about the life span of the average Baby Boomer. They have seen the integration of television into day-to-day—now moment-to-moment—lives. They experience growing reliance on digital communications to stay in touch with the world. They have seen men walk on the moon, dive to the depths of the ocean, and explore the universe through the eye of the Hubble Telescope. They have watched telephones lose their cords, computers lose their bulk, and video and still-shot cameras lose their film. They have gone from LP's to AM/FM to 8-Track to cassettes to CD's to live streaming sound and picture in search of the perfect song.

Now think about the life span of the average Gen X or Gen Y individual. They, too, were born into a world that was changing quickly. In their earliest years they went from standard color TV to high resolution to HDTV. From wide screens to flat screens to screens that can bring television and videos into the palms of their hands as they use their phones for entertainment. They have grown up in a world where geo-political boundaries change overnight and where yesterday's deadly diseases are less lethal and are closer to being curable.

In this world of life-altering change that occurs at the speed of tomorrow, complex systems are being called upon to adapt more quickly and also to a wider variety of challenges and opportunities than ever before. From individual families who deal with these phenomena at the personal and interpersonal level, to neighborhoods, communities, and organizations; to government and educational institutions, there is a unified need. This need is for new tools and perspectives to help build relationships, productivity, and commitments required to sustain life—to find fitness in today's environment.

How can that be done when today's environment changes before the completion of a scan to identify what to plan? How can anyone plan for a tomorrow that may or may not look like today? How can people account for change and new technology when there's no way to know what that might be?

Today individuals cry out for ways to deal with the complex changes they face. Even the most traditionally steady systems have been thrown far from equilibrium and seek greater balance. Governmental institutions, public education, health care, and our financial systems—all exist in a precarious balance, weighing new demands against traditional approaches that seem to be less effective today.

Think about infrastructures such as public roads and highways, electrical power grids, and public transportation struggle to serve the ever-growing demands. Sustainability has become a critical watchword for tomorrow, even as individuals and communities struggle to maintain today's systems.

At all levels, people seek appropriate answers to these challenges. Responses must continue to meet the needs of the system, wherever people stand and however they seek to help. This demands that responses are sensitive, flexible, energetic, and rigorous.

Sensitivity to Overall Conditions

People need to be attentive to and in tune with their environment and the patterns around them. They must be observant over time, reflecting on what they see and how they experience the world. Both collectively and individually people have to stay in touch with the environment, collecting information about what is happening across the landscape, and gauging its potential impact on their lives.

"As my own neighborhood changes, I am aware of shifts. I know who moves in and out around me. I pay attention to how people respond to each other. In the same way I watch the landscape of my profession. What's new? Who is doing what? How do people respond? I remain sensitive to the signal fires around me.

~Royce

Flexibility in Our Responses

As people move toward their goals, they cannot lose sight of their original purposes. This requires them to remain flexible in their responses. For instance, if someone's real purpose as a community member is to provide connections across internal boundaries, he might help establish neighborhood watches and organize a local celebration of National Night Out. He might set up phone trees for sharing information.

As the community becomes more diverse and more technologically cued in, he would need to think about communication differently. He might explore using social networking as an effective way to share information. The point is this: he must find flexible and responsive ways to continue in purpose.

Energy to Meet Challenges

Any response to change must maintain energy, drive, and enthusiasm to succeed. Individuals must remain engaged. They cannot shut the door and ignore the winds outside. They cannot withdraw and expect that others will handle what needs to be done. They cannot carry the burden of the entire world on their shoulders and expect to maintain strength over time. Sustaining energy requires vigorous collaboration in a shared quest to succeed. Mutual support and encouragement are the key.

Rigor in Our Methods

Individuals will organize with diligence and thoughtful regard for the task at hand to reach their goals. They maintain focus and adhere to standards and shared expectations. In their work lives they often have regulations and operational standards set by their employers. It's critical that they seek similar agreements about performance and work in their other communities as well.

Even as an individual considers personal challenges and growth, if she does not move forward with rigor and accountability, her performance may or may not take her along the path to where she wants to go. As she expands her circle of influence and begins to work with others in her community, any lack of clarity about where they are going, how they will get there, or how they will inform each other about their chosen path will lead to confusion and conflict. Energy and time can be wasted; relationships can be damaged; opportunities can be lost. They must know what the signal fires mean and must be constant in watching for their flares. This requires clarity about goals as well as clarity about choosing the path toward those goals. What is important and how can choices be made accordingly?

This level of commitment calls for new tools to see and understand the patterns of life and interaction. An exploration of new and exciting possibilities can create a level of functioning equal to the challenges ahead.

Essentially three questions emerge from this exploration.

- How can we see and identify the many signal fires around our horizon?

- How can we make sense of the signal fires to take action that moves us toward fitness?

- How do we gather feedback that informs our next steps—which entails seeing and identifying the next set of signal fires?

The Adaptive Action Cycle

A model for planning and implementing desired change has emerged in human systems dynamics. It is called Adaptive Action and has been used to facilitate change in a wide range of systems. The methodology consists of three questions, simplified versions of the essential questions listed above:

- What?
- So What?
- Now What?

These straightforward questions inform decision making and action by capturing good information about patterns in the system. They help us, recognize and understand those patterns before we make decisions about shaping those patterns of interaction and behavior. These questions allow us to think about change in a different way. They provide a framework for action that is **sensitive** to changes in the environment; helps us respond in **flexible** ways; engages individuals and groups in ongoing, **energetic** work that supports focused activity; and enables **rigorous** application of a shared process to move toward group goals.They help us move forward in small, iterative steps as we make sense of our worlds even as we have impact on that world.

What?

This phase helps planners see and identify the multitude of signal fires around their horizon. In this phase data is used to describe presenting issues and environmental factors. Questions set the stage for shared or individual inquiries. Careful collection of information and thoughtful reflection about responses to those questions allow clear definitions of next steps to move forward.

- In the tragedy and pain following the terrorist attacks of September 11, 2001, the shared American response was magnified by the fact that such a level of violence was rare in the collective experience. While it would be no less tragic or painful in any other country, the general cultural response may be different. The attack took on additional meaning for Americans because it was so far from their experience.

- The international interest and excitement about World Cup Soccer is played out each summer as countries compete, sending their most talented and able athletes to the competition. In the summer of 2010, when Spain won the Cup, the celebration of Spanish national pride reflected the importance of this victory across that country.

- Faith-based celebrations are fashioned on both the shared meaning of the holy day, but also on the cultural expectations and experiences of the various groups within that community. For instance, among Christians, many different traditions mark the birth of Christ, and each of them has powerful meaning for the faithful.

- No two families are alike. Think about the roles of the parents; expectations about birth order, gender, behavior and performance, and relationships. All are influenced by the meaning each unique group of individuals brings to their interactions with each other and with their greater community.

Whether dealing with challenges at work, in the community, or even in their individual lives, people ask questions. Questions are key to being sensitive to the changes in light and dark, pressure and resistance, and mingling and isolation. Those questions might look like the following.

- What is the current situation?

- What patterns of behavior can be found?

- What culture has emerged?

- What impacts, whether positive or negative, have resulted?

- What additional information is needed about the environment?

- What has been done so far about the situation and what have been the results?

- What needs to be discovered about each group of players?

- What do players think about the overall situation?

- What is anyone doing about the situation?

- And so on ...

So What?

During the *So What?* phase, data is analyzed to find and name system-wide patterns of interaction and behavior. These patterns help explain the environment and how groups or individuals can move forward. This is the time to make sense of the signal fires, to take action, and move toward fitness.

People rely on what they know and can measure through science and technology; they then make sense of it through memory, tradition, and myth. This is what it is to *make meaning* of events, information, and relationships. Both individually and at the collective level, people interpret their worlds through myriad screens of experience.

Groups and individuals make meaning of their worlds as they consider the events and activities around them in light of what they know and believe. The meaning they derive informs the actions they take. Experiencing the events in the examples above, individuals and groups responded in varying ways, grounded in their own beliefs, experiences, and myth.

- After September 11, 2001, many Americans responded by immediately expressing strong nationalism. People all over the world rallied in support and began to cope with increased security measures as they traveled. When the United States took military action in the Middle East, international opinions of American chauvinism became evident.

- Soccer teams return to their countries amidst varying responses as they are eliminated through the World Cup tournament. Some return as heroes, defeated but proud of their commitment. Others return defeated and shunned for their lack of success and their failure to represent their countries well. The value and meaning assigned to the World Cup by a country will guide how their team is greeted as it returns from competition—win or lose.

- The ways people celebrate holy days in the various faith communities often influences the markets in those societies. Manufacturers, retailers, and entertainers use the traditions of their own communities to prepare and sell specialty foods, gifts, decorations, and even music.

- How individuals are raised will influence the traditions, roles, and expectations they may carry into their own adult relationships. How they share and blend their traditions in new communities is informed and influenced by the ways in which they make meaning of their own experiences.

In the *So What?* phase, questions help examine what all the data means and what steps should be taken.

- Given the data, what needs to be accomplished and how can that happen?

- What patterns can take the place of those that are less productive? What patterns should remain and be amplified?

- What conditions in the system are generating those patterns?

- What options exist for taking action to shift a pattern?

- What steps will shift conditions within the system?

- Who will be involved and in what capacities?

- What resources are needed; how will they be acquired?

- What is the desired outcome?

- Now, go ahead. Develop and implement your plan. Marshall your resources and begin to take intentional steps toward your goals.

Now What?

This phase provides the opportunity to pause, take a breath, and look at what has been accomplished. It is a time to identify what works and feed that information back into the system, informing the next step.

The steps that change the system shift boundaries; alter relationships, connections, and expectations; and work with differences. In the end stronger relationships may be formed, old relationships may be abandoned, and new patterns will emerge.

Following from the four examples above, actions at the individual and group level led individuals and communities to different patterns and challenges.

- Airlines have continued expanded security measures adopted after September 11, 2001, and some individuals have significantly altered their own travel rituals and practices in response to that.

- The national traditions of how international soccer team members are revered are slower to change, but at the individual level, each team member makes personal decisions about continuing to participate or not. Some of those decisions may be influenced by the ways in which they have been honored—or not —as representatives of their countries.

- Vendors, families, groups, and individuals make choices about how to celebrate the next holiday, based on a number of factors. Manufacturers and retailers look at sales and determine what worked and what did not. Entertainers know whether their particular brand of entertainment was popular by demand or whether they need to look for a different approach in the next holiday season.

- Some individuals carry on strong patterns— traditions and expectations—they learn from their families; others make choices to shift those patterns and/or create new ones different from their families. Individual choice depends on a number of factors unique to each situation.

In this phase of the Adaptive Action Cycle, questions now focus on what has been done, how the system has moved, and the current status. It is often at this time that people become more conscious and more intentional in their adaptations. Choices get reinforced, and learning becomes solidified. It is also time for more data collection.

- How did the system respond?

- What were the surprises?

- What was the greatest learning? What was the greatest challenge?

- When did the patterns shift?

- How did the actual achievements compare to individual's expectations?

- What should be done differently next time?

- What was learned?

- What was changed?

- What new questions emerged?

You may have noticed something interesting here: The *Now What?* has turned into another *What?* That is the nature of the cycle. You identify the issue or concern. You name and come to understand the patterns that are present and the conditions that generate those patterns. Then, because you have this deeper level of understanding, you are able to make choices and take steps to shift the system and see the impact of those actions.

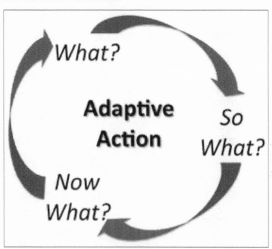

Now, go back to your issue or concern and see what has changed. If the situation has shifted for the better, celebrate your success and see what needs to be changed next. If it has not changed, or if it has gotten worse, then go back to the beginning, collect data that exists at that point, and see what is possible —start the cycle on its next iteration.

Know that success in the Adaptive Action Cycle is about inquiry. It's about what you learn and how you use that as your next signal fire. It is also important to note that the Adaptive Action Cycle offers benefits at multiple levels.

- **It works at different scales of human systems.** The model is applicable in the larger scope of setting direction for a whole organization, or it can be scaled down to consider the actions of an individual. In the explanation, the examples provided glimpses into global, national, community, family, and individual experiences.

- **It formalizes planning.** This process can be used formally as a foundation for long-range, strategic, or personal action planning. The adaptive cycle includes documentation and ritual around data collection, analysis, and implementation.

- **It helps day-to-day problem solving.** The model can be used informally as challenges arise. At any point an individual can stop and ask *What? So What?* or *Now What?* as they move from one decision to the next.

- **It generates more questions.** Because all systems are in constant motion, emergent patterns will trigger more questions than answers. Today's questions always lead to new answers and the next question.

- **You can never get stuck:** Wherever the process stalls just asking, *What?* will start another iteration and move the process forward again.

The Legacy Sustainability Model

Trying to bring about significant, sustainable change in patterns of behavior and interaction is no easy task, even when people know what needs to be done. What is more difficult is being able to make careful, sensible choices in the day-to-day, moment-to-moment times of life. The Legacy Sustainability Model, the second tool, offers a blueprint for building lasting change across a system.

Sustainability requires that a system be strong enough at its root to allow for flexible, adaptive responses to the changing world. As you engage in Radical Inquiry, it will be critical to be strong in your purposes and beliefs, even as you remain flexible and responsive to your environment. The Legacy Sustainability Model frames this level of flexible strength, by introducing seven elements for you to consider as you move toward your goals.

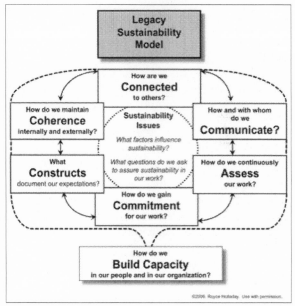

Each element is explained below, followed by an example of how one person, *Richard,* used this model to sustain his own change efforts.

One of Richard's simple rules was to maintain a healthy lifestyle. He had thought about this for some time and was concerned for his well-being and what he was modeling for his children. The time was now.

How are we Connected to others? is about contacts and the quality of relationships. How people connect with each other is an important element in their ability to respond. Another aspect of connections is self-awareness—what information do you have about your own performance, needs, skills, and relationships? In addition, you move from understanding yourself to connecting with others and with the world at large. Connections help you see and understand similarities, differences, and relationships—the patterns of your life. These connections become the anchors that hold you steady in the turbulence of change.

Richard made sure that the people in his life were well aware of his commitment to lose weight. He talked with his family, the members of his carpool, and others he thought needed to know about the choices he was making.

How do we Communicate? is about sharing and collecting data and the open, multiple channels and feedback loops that give you information about your effort. Communication may be formal or informal, but it must be open and frequent to engage others. You need to know what is important and what you need. You have to gather information about your world. For example: What opportunities and barriers are out there? What supports do you need? What supports do you have? What feedback is available? All of these questions are about establishing solid, clear, and consistent communication messages and contacts with individuals who are important to you.

> *Richard shared his diet and exercise routine with family members to be sure they understood what he should and should not be doing. He set up regular appointments to talk with his dietician and the doctor. He kept a journal to track and remind himself about his progress.*

How do we Continuously Assess our work? is the ongoing collection and examination of information about your performance, in light of desired patterns. Initially, your performance is measured against a baseline or starting line. As your activity increases, and progress is made, comparisons are taken against the last measure. This is how you know how well you are doing. You track progress as well as share and ask for specific and honest feedback. Charts, images, journals, and other tools communicate new patterns as they begin to emerge.

> *Richard's journal of his exercise and eating habits helped him see patterns of change as they showed in his notes. Additionally he weighed himself weekly, recording and tracking his progress.*

How do we gain Commitment for our work? helps others understand and value what you offer them so they involve themselves in your success. They contribute to your work and support you through to its conclusion. The purpose of this element is to invite others to champion, promote, and exercise their influence to help you reach your goals. Commitment is also reciprocal as you express your commitment to partners and others in your world.

Richard engaged his wife and family to support his efforts. He shared with them his fears about his health and his commitment to be healthier and more active in their lives. In return they committed to support him and help him remain accountable for his actions.

What Constructs document our expectations? are all the pieces, ideas, theories, models, and resources that comprise and support your planning and implementation of change. You establish processes and structures that must be strong enough to support you, even as they are flexible enough to allow you to shift over time. Your constructs may include stated intentions, formal and informal plans, your decision-making processes, and expectations and goal statements. They are also the ways you organize your life to make room for and secure new patterns. For example, how often and deeply do you journal about who you are and the experiences that shape your life? What are your goals and how do you track your progress toward them? Your vision statements and images, music, or experiences that give your goals meaning become the constructs of the new patterns you seek in your life.

Richard's journal, weekly weight record, and printed diet were the foundations that helped him remain steadfast in his efforts. Three times each week, he went to the gym at work establishing an exercise schedule. At the gym, he engaged a trainer as an additional support for his workouts.

How do we maintain Coherence internally and externally? refers to how the parts of your life align with the patterns you seek to create. Internal coherence is about sharing goals, united purpose, and common meanings that guide your action. When your life is coherent, patterns tend to be in synch, and they support each other as well. In Radical Inquiry, coherence refers to how well the conditions you set align with the patterns you want to generate. Does what you say match what you do? External coherence reflects your fitness in the greater environment. How well does what you want align with the conditions you set? Do the people you hang out with have goals and interests that are coherent with what you say you want?

> *Richard knew that he had never been a highly active or competitive athlete, so he was careful to design an exercise regimen that matched his interests and skill levels. Similarly, he built his diet around foods he knew he liked so he would eat well and not be tempted to cheat.*

How do we build our Capacity? ensures you have what you need in terms of resources and support, processes and skills, and information. This is a critical piece that not only adds understanding but also supports for your ongoing growth and learning. Individual capacity has to do with your own strength and insights about the changes you want and the work you have to do to get there. It has to do with your ability and willingness to remain strong and true to your goals, while remaining flexible enough to respond to changes that would otherwise limit your success.

> *Over time Richard increased his physical stamina and actually came to enjoy fresh and healthy cuisine. His understanding of the relationship between nutrition and his own health increased his commitment to eat well. As an added bonus,*

Richard eventually lost enough weight that he no longer felt self-conscious wearing the shorts and tee-shirts he felt most comfortable in.

Each of these elements exerts strong influence on the sustainability of the change you are working to bring about. AND they exert strong influence on each other as you build your own systems of change and adaptation. The quality of your connections depends on the effectiveness of your communications and your capacity to share ideas. Constructs help you see coherence, support you in formulating your communications, and garner commitment because people see how committed you are. As you can see each element is similarly interdependent with the others and together they create a network of support for sustainability.

Conclusion

Remember there are no right or wrong answers. It is about fit—more explicitly it is about YOUR fit in the environment where you live, work, and play. Not only do you get to make the decisions, this is where you are the expert!

• You remain sensitive to your environment so you can respond to challenges in flexible ways. You also use energy pursuing change in ways that maintain your integrity.

• You use the Adaptive Action Cycle to gather information to help you see and influence your own conditions for success.

• You build a network of accountability by applying elements of the Legacy Sustainability Model.

CHAPTER 4

All of this is to say you are the leader of your change effort and endeavors. You are diligent in watching for and interpreting the signal fires and you rally the energy, time, and other resources to move forward on the journey toward tomorrow.

I am wondering if the adaptive learning cycle is about my personal fit with change - how do we collaborate

Doesn't this mean we will all be handling/ managing change individually?

CHAPTER 5

"Things do not change. We change."
~Henry David Thoreau

There are those who believe that Henry David Thoreau was an individual who never stopped looking for the truth. In his writings, lifestyle, and other choices, he made statements about living life creatively and independently. Always asking questions, he sought meaning for his life in his chosen surroundings. Was he, too, on a journey of Radical Inquiry?

Chapter 4 guided us through the use of two powerful tools to help us in our Radical Inquiry. The Adaptive Action Cycle allows us to understand the thought processes that lead to decision making and planning; the Legacy Sustainability Model articulates our connections to the world and our capacity to move forward. In this chapter we will describe the ways these concepts come alive for us every day.

You Are Your Own Signal Fire

Changing your own behavior is the challenge, and that is hard to do unless you become much more self-aware than you are now or than most people are about what counterproductive behaviors are, how they are reinforced, and what they mean. You have to inquire into how you weigh data, make decisions, and what exactly is happening as you respond. Only then can you intentionally interrupt those old patterns and formulate new ones.

Now people have been successfully making changes in their lives—including you—every minute of every day without having read this book and without delving into how you made those decisions and how people responded. You may not have known anything about *patterns of behavior* and yet you were able to make significant change in your life.

So why are these tools and concepts important?

They are important because these ideas explain the *why* about what you have to do and help make your actions more planned and intentional. They also allow you to be more mindful about choices you make and the implications of those choices for you and those around you. This book provides a roadmap and tools for bringing about the changes you want to have

and a clearer grasp of your ability to choose and the choices you make.

The three tools that have been introduced to you so far—Simple Rules, the Adaptive Action Cycle, and the Legacy Sustainability Model—allow you to be more specific and focused. Together these tools set the stage as they help you:

- Articulate what is important; what matters most

- Identify patterns to change

- Name the outcomes you want

- Map out actions to move you toward your goals

- Engage others to support and reinforce the change

- Find ways to sustain the new patterns over time

We offer a process you and anyone else can use to bring about this level of change in your life. It can be taught and learned, and it's portable enough to be used in all areas of your life. Radical Inquiry is the process that can light your next signal fire.

Engaging in Radical Inquiry

When you seek to understand and change your life for the better, you recognize and set the conditions for learning and transformation. Old habits and ways of thinking about what is best and which way to turn cannot bring about reflective, intentional change in your complex environments.

As a result, you need to stand in a place of inquiry, asking informed questions that help you see the patterns that make up your life. It may sound foolish to talk about asking questions when you are supposed to know the answers about yourself; however, you can appreciate that there are parts of your own personality and behavior that even you cannot readily see. And so you inquire.

Radical Inquiry is a personal process that takes you down your own unique path reflecting on or answering a series of questions to clarify your thinking. Then it guides you to use those answers to sort through options about what you can do, what you need to do, what you might like to do, and what is possible in creating the patterns you want to see.

Remember that standing in inquiry is also about being open to surprises along the way. It is important that when you engage in personal Radical Inquiry, you do so with an open mind that allows you to see new possibilities and then remain available to the unexpected.

Note that you don't have to shift everything in your life to bring about significant changes. Remember that a change in any one part of your life will cause adjustments in other areas as well. For instance, when you want to change something like a propensity for procrastination, you can shift that pattern to do things over time rather than at the last minute. Perhaps you can create an alternate deadline for yourself that is, in reality, a week before the actual deadline.

This might also shift the quality of work you do. Without the pressure of an approaching deadline, you may identify and commit more resources to the project and create a better outcome. You may establish time for additional review and reflection. You may even have time to take a deep breath.

Additionally if you find that it serves you well, such a shift might alter how you think about time in other areas of your life. It could change your relationships because you're better able to maintain consistent contacts with others when you are not always fighting the specter of a deadline. This is part

of the unexpected consequences we have warned you about.

The Process of Radical Inquiry

Focus your Radical Inquiry on one area, deciding first what you want to change. Pick one small change; don't try to do it all at once. When it comes to Radical Inquiry, it's not only day-by-day change; it is also a challenge-by-challenge effort. It's an iterative process where you will make a change that will cause other changes, which, in turn, will bring about other changes. Stop periodically to see where you stand. Maybe each year as you think about New Year's resolutions, ask yourself whether your simple rules are still consistent with what is important to you. Ask yourself if you are still on the path to a sustainable and productive life.

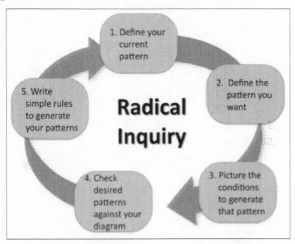

There are probably as many ways to conduct a personal inquiry as there are people on the planet. What you will find here is a set of steps. Please feel free to modify them if you need to—as long as you get to the same general destination. The critical pieces are where you start—right here and now—and where you want to be—working on the patterns of your choosing. Your route is a very personal path you develop as you continue to grow and learn.

Use the diagram below (or in the companion journal that goes with this book) as you work through the example Radical Inquiry on the next pages. We have outlined the steps, questions, and considerations that may help you think through your own issue or challenge.

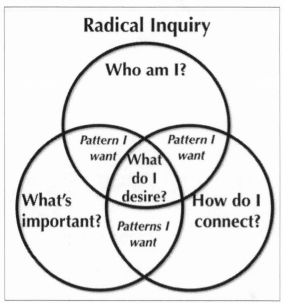

Step 1—Define your current patterns. The first stage of a Radical Inquiry is to define the patterns you currently have in your life. Remember that patterns are the themes or constants that characterize your life. You may wish to return to the three foundational questions presented previously:

• Who am I?

- What's important?

- How do I connect to others?

No matter how badly things seem to be going, there are at least one or two current patterns that are worth retaining in your life—celebrate those and hang onto them.

The following actions will help you see and define your current patterns.

- Name the current life patterns you can identify for yourself. Think about what your current patterns are and what they create for you. Now remember: you don't want to identify every single pattern that characterizes your life. Choose one area of life where you truly want to focus your energies and think abut those specific patterns.

- Ask trusted friends and colleagues how they characterize or describe you in the area of life you choose as your focus. Remember you are sincerely reaching out to credible sources with positive, productive intentions, and their responses should be a reflection of that. Remain open. Don't try to defend or explain, just sit still and listen. Ask them to help you think about specific behaviors and/or incidences they are using as indicators in this discussion. Then think about those behaviors and incidences and see what is common among them. What was the overall outcome or consequence of various events? What one or two words most thoroughly describe the patterns that come up in these discussions?

- Start a journal to keep track of the patterns you see. If you have kept a journal in the past, go back and see what patterns emerge now that you are looking for them. If you have used another method of collecting and tracking thoughts, ideas, inspirations, musings, and changes that have been part of your life, go back to that, too. Now, what do you see? Where are your entries consistently upbeat and positive? Where are they not? How do you describe your relationships? Is there consistency in your priorities and decisions? Is there a pattern to the times your decision making has been out of synch with what you really wanted? What do you think about those patterns and how would you name or characterize them?

- Be sure to consider your behaviors in areas relative to the one you choose to focus on—and on areas that might not seem related. Again, this is a Radical Inquiry—while there is a process in place, you want to remain open to information and data coming from unexpected, random, and surprising places.

For instance, if you choose to focus your attention on patterns around "Money," you will pretty naturally focus your attention on your patterns around earning and spending. Remember to think also about patterns around how you save money and how you consider money as a factor in your life. Do the television shows you watch and newspapers you read influence your thinking about money? How did people around you think about money and deal with money issues as you were growing up? What might be your unspoken simple rules that would effect how you think about money today? What other area in your life yields similar patterns? What would help you think about these patterns?

Step 2 – Define the patterns you want. What is it you really want in life and what are the patterns of behavior and interaction that will get you there? Think about those patterns that you see in others. Are there patterns you want to copy? Are there patterns you want to avoid at all costs? List even those patterns that might not seem related but that somehow feel important here. Whatever they are, get very

specific and name them, listing the discreet behaviors that will add up to those patterns over time.

For instance if you want to change your decisions about money, what patterns will most likely emerge with that? Patterns of saving? Patterns of careful spending? Increased earning? Conservation? Each of those patterns will be made up of some different and some overlapping behaviors. Make a list and begin thinking about individual behaviors and patterns. Brainstorm all the ideas you can. Remember that you don't have to do them all—you are just brainstorming for later decision making. Challenge yourself to list a number of descriptors to increase the options for consideration as you move to action.

Behaviors Related to My Patterns

Patterns of Saving

- *Put money in a savings account out of each paycheck.*

- *Use a container to hold extra change each day. Every 3 months empty the container and put the money you've collected into the bank.*

- *Talk to a financial advisor; see if you are using the most productive ways to save.*

Patterns of Careful Spending

- *Never go shopping without a list.*

- *Use coupons.*

- *Check prices and compare quality.*

- *Look for end-of-season or closeout sales.*

- *Find ways to purchase items at wholesale prices when possible.*

Patterns of Increased Earning

- *Identify possible second jobs or additional sources of income.*

- *Look for sources of passive income.*

- *Decide if you need further training in your own field or in another field to increase your earning power.*

Patterns of Conservation

- *Turn off the lights and electronic equipment in your house when you are not using them.*

- *Make sure you have no leaky faucets or other utilities.*

- *Recycle whatever you can, whether it is paper, plastic, metal, glass, as well as any old clothes, household items, and furniture.*

Step 3 – Build a "picture" of the conditions that will generate those patterns. This part of the process serves two purposes. First, it helps you visualize a fairly abstract idea as a *thing* you can touch and change. Second, it serves as a record of your thinking process.

1. Draw three overlapping circles to form a Venn diagram like the one earlier in this chapter (or use this one and write your answers in the book).

2. In the center, where all three circles overlap, put the one or two words that most clearly describe what it is you want. Think carefully and make that descriptor broad enough that it can include all the patterns you have named in this one area of your life.

So, using the example about money, you may want to focus on Wealth or Being Worry Free or some other descriptor. Play with this term; it only has to make sense to you--no one else. Maybe the term is Eccentric, meaning you want to be able to buy whatever whimsy you want so people will say you are "eccentric." Maybe you are saving for a particular item or event—then put that in the middle.

3. In the top circle, answer the question, "Who are you?" in the context of what you want. This question really is about what draws you in or would hold you in this area of life. What is it? or How do you want to be in this area of life?

    Maybe in the area of money, what draws you there is Security or Freedom or being in the A-Crowd. Maybe it is about being able to do something special—take a trip or buy something you want. Whatever it is, put it down—this is just for you.

4. In the lower left circle, put a descriptor of what is important to you in this area. What is the one critical factor or concept related to the idea that will influence your decisions?

    How will you make decisions about money? If Security is in your top circle, it may be that the thing that is most important in that context is whether or not what you are considering is necessary for life then you might put Need in that circle to say that all decisions will be based on need. If Freedom occupies the top circle, perhaps Desire is a better choice here.

5. In the lower right circle, describe the ways you want to connect with others about this issue. What rules will inform your decisions? How will you communicate to others about your decisions? How will you gather feedback and judge your success?

When you think about money, you may want to use Budget to describe how you connect. A budget sets the expectations about what and where you can spend. It gives you a way to communicate with others about your spending. Judging your actual spending against the budget can give you feedback about your performance. If instead you state, Never touch the principle, that identifies a different way of managing your finances and your values.

Step 4 – Check your desired patterns against the diagram. Once the Venn diagram is complete, go back and see if the words you put down in the circles work together to create the patterns you want and lead you to the spot in the center, which is your goal. If they look like they would, then you're finished. If they don't, go back and identify concepts that do work together more effectively. Maybe one of the circles doesn't quite fit what you want. Maybe your patterns aren't really coherent with each other or with what you wrote in the middle of the circle.

What kinds of patterns will be generated when you think about security and make all your decisions based on need? Which patterns would be generated if you think about security and use a budget to build that? What kinds of patterns will you see if you budget your money in terms of need? Alternatively, what kinds of patterns will be generated when you think about freedom and make all your decisions based on desire or want? Which patterns would be generated if you think

about freedom and use your assets to build and sustain that? What kinds of patterns will you see if you access your money based upon your latest must-have?

Step 5 – Write your simple rules and test them. Now you are ready to write your simple rules. Ask yourself, "What are the 5–7 broad rules you could write that would, if you followed them, shape your behavior according to the descriptors you have written?" Start by writing at least one rule for each of the circles. Remember the guidelines about simple rules you read earlier.

- Keep the list short. You cannot focus or remember more than about 5–7 rules at a time.

- Keep the rules simple. None of them should have lots of qualifiers or *ifs, ands, or buts* in them.

- You need a rule that guides your behavior for each of the three circles.

- Start each rule with a verb and make it a positive statement. Always say what you need to do, rather than what not to do. You want the rules to tell you how to act or what to do. It's not enough just to tell you what not to do.

- Remember that the simple rules should be both generalizable across similar situations and scalable to higher and lower levels.

What rule will help you focus on Security, since that is what draws you to this idea? What rule will help you focus on Need? What rule will help you focus on Budget? What other rules are necessary to get to Being Worry Free as you posted it in the center of the diagram?

Some sample simple rules for this might include:

Know what you need to know. *This will build security by helping you prepare for risk and by helping you anticipate challenges or dangers that might be coming at you. It is generalizable in that it can be used in other areas of your life. This is also scalable in that it can contribute to how you pay attention to others in your life and what you try to know about your community and what's happening on a national or global scale.*

Take care of yourself and others. *This gets at the issues of need. What do you need in terms of spending/money issues? What do you need for other areas: entertainment, health, education, training, etc.? So it is generalizable. It is scalable because it calls you to think about others at the local, community, and global levels.*

Give everything its due. *This will help you think about what is in the budget and what can be spent where. Again the statement is generalizable because you want to give other things what they are due—enough attention to the people around you, enough thought about your life and future, enough other resources to maintain health and home. At the same time you can think about it at several levels—giving your spouse or family what they are due; paying your taxes; contributing to the community—making it scalable.*

There is an interesting point here you may have noticed yourself: If you chose *freedom* instead of *security*, these same simple rules would still apply. What would be different is how you interpret and operationalize them. This tells us that your simple rules are not necessarily unique to you; what is unique is how you define and use them in your life. You and I could conceivably have the same set of simple rules

and lead extremely diverse existences if our values were poles apart. This process is about how we create our own simple rules and manifest them in our own lives. *That is Radical!* Read this second possible interpretation of the simple rules from the example above.

> ***Know what you need to know.*** *Your freedom may depend upon your understanding and knowledge of finances and resources available to you; fluctuations in the markets and global economies; political and environmental challenges; and to be prepared for shifts that may occur. This includes recognizing and appreciating others in your life, the community you live in and the world at large.*

> ***Take care of yourself and others.*** *You may indeed be fortunate enough to be able to have and do those things that support you and give you joy. What can you do for others in your life? How can you contribute and give back to your neighbors and environment? What will you do to support others across town or across the nation?*

> ***Give everything its due.*** *Not only can you meet your personal and professional commitments, you can also maintain the worthy efforts of others. Will you set up an endowment at the local university? Fund national efforts on preventing domestic violence? Volunteer to build a school in a developing country? How does your simple rule support you as the individual, the whole, and the greater whole?*

The crucial thing is whether or not the simple rules you choose can be applied to help you create the patterns you want in any area in your life. If you live out these simple rules in relationships, in your work, in business dealings, in your community work ... would they generate patterns you want to live by in all those areas as well?

Remember that you can't know everything you need to know about the future. What you want is a list that is good enough for this place and time. If the rules seem to generalize and scale now—that's good enough. If you find later that they don't work so well in another area, then you can make that shift at that time.

Integrating Your Radical Inquiry

Identify one pattern you want to shift, and make plans to change it. This next set of steps is one of the most difficult, and it is critical to long-term success. It's where you use the Adaptive Action Cycle and the Legacy Sustainability Model to integrate your Radical Inquiry into your life.

What?—Look carefully at all the patterns you've identified relative to the issue you chose to address. You have to select one pattern to tackle specifically—you can't do them all. Particularly at the beginning of a self-improvement process, it's easy to be excited and motivated and feel like almost anything is possible. The key is to be realistic.

The truth is that we really can't do everything at once, and trying to do too much will have two impacts. First, it will dilute both your focus and your energy. Second, if you try to work on several patterns at once, you run the risk of allowing yourself to become overwhelmed by the scope of what has to be done. Just wait and see the impact you bring about first and then decide what needs to be done next.

Once you identify the pattern you want to change, you have to collect all the information you can about that pattern—what events or situations in your environment trigger those patterns for you? How do others see the pattern emerge? Do those closest to you

see it differently than how others see it? Does the pattern change, depending on where you are and what you are doing?

Be sure to include the elements of the Legacy Sustainability Model in your questions. How are you connected to others? How and what do you communicate? What measurement data is available? What is the level of commitment from others in your life? What constructs will help you carry this out? Is this coherent with other areas in your life? What is your capacity for doing this work?

> *Go back to the example about money. Looking at the patterns, you might review each one, consider the impact it has, and decide that the pattern of how you spend money is what you want to work on. What you would do is then collect all the information you can about how you spend money. Keep a journal to track your spending. Note where and when you are likely to overspend or under-spend. Note where you are careful and thoughtful in your spending and where you are impulsive. Note which expenditures are based upon need and which are about desire? How do your friends and family make their decisions? How do their decisions influence your own? What other questions can you ask yourself about your spending patterns?*

So What? Then you have to analyze all the information you have collected. Consider the information in terms of what it means to you now physically, socially, emotionally, and psychologically. Asking *So What?* helps you reflect on how that information influences what you think and how you behave. What part of it makes you happy or silly or hopeful? What part makes you uncomfortable or angry or depressed?

What does this information mean in your world? This reflection focuses on what you can discern about the ways in which others in your world are influenced or challenged by these patterns and what that means in your life. How do friends, family, and colleagues influence your behavior and/or thinking? Based on the data you have collected in response to the questions about the Legacy elements, what do you now know about the potential for sustainability?

> *What meaning can you make from your current patterns of spending? What do you see as the greatest impact or as the gravest impact? What have you learned that can influence your spending? How can this help you make better decisions?*

After you have done this level of exploration and questioning, you begin to formulate a plan for moving forward. Looking at what needs to be changed might be balanced by what is already working pretty well, so map steps that take advantage of your assets. Also make sure your steps let you behave according to your simple rules, taking into account the three circles in the Venn diagram.

One last action you will need to take in this phase is to decide how you will judge your success. What will be the criteria by which you will decide you have changed your patterns in the way you need them to change? What will you see in your own behavior? What will you see happening with the people around you?

In other words, based upon what you have decided is important to you, how you want to shift your pattern and what your goal is, how will you know when you have gotten there? You must establish these indicators firmly in your mind because those are the measures

you will be watching for. Make sure that the measures you name will be impacted by the strategies you choose—both at the level of individual actions or behaviors and at the level of the overall patterns you are creating. Finally, identify a timeframe for when you will check in to see how you are moving forward.

Remember that you identified the following simple rules about money.

- *Know what you need to know.*

- *Take care of your self and others.*

- *Give everything its due.*

Strategies for shifting your patterns of spending to support a goal of security could include the following as an example.

- *Slow down and before you put something into your shopping cart (real or virtual), stop and ask yourself three questions. If the answer to any one of them is "No" then put the item back and make the purchase at a later date.*

  - *Do you really need this? (Simple rule #2)*

  - *Is this the best value for the price? (Simple rule #1)*

  - *Do I really have the money to purchase this at this time? (Simple rule #3)*

Measures you might select, based on what you want to accomplish and based on the strategies you set, could include the following, as you set the date for a reflective check in 3 months.

- *Impulse spending decreases by more than half.*

- *Household spending and expenses decrease by a given amount.*

- *You live inside the budget with no overages for 3 months in a row.*

Now What? Once you identify your strategies, you put them into action and see what happens. Maintain your journaling to watch patterns and note whether the strategies become easier as time goes on. At what point do the strategies become habits, as opposed to "steps" you have to remember to take? When do you see different patterns emerging? Or do you see new patterns at all? Look around and check out what is happening in your larger world. Are others relating to you differently? Is your behavior being reinforced in different ways? Where do you stand on the Legacy elements of sustainability?

Based on your observations and data collection, you may find you have not been as successful as you would have liked. Don't beat yourself up. Instead, determine what else you can do. There may be a need to choose a new pattern to address, if your data leads you to believe that this one is too entrenched; or didn't really get to the essence of your concern as well as you thought it would. Perhaps your strategies were not effective—or you were not effective in implementing them.

You can name any number of reasons and excuses. What is critical is that you answer as honestly as possible. Not reaching your full goal is not a failure— it is merely a call to return to the *"What?"* stage and explore other options that have the potential to move you forward.

In fact, that is the same option you have if you achieve or exceed all the goals you set forth. In that case, the question at the beginning shifts from "What do I need to do with this pattern?" to "What other patterns or actions are causing me difficulty and what do I want to do about those?" This becomes, then, the trigger for the first step in the next cycle of Adaptive Action, and the next phase in the process of your Radical Inquiry. The elements of the Legacy Model

to move you through a life of sustainable reflection and self-improvement.

Conclusion

This, then, is the essence of a Radical Inquiry. It is an honest and thorough examination of one area of your life, with the goal of finding the most effective and efficient ways of bringing about meaningful and lasting change.

In the next chapter, we outline the process we worked through to develop the simple rules we used in our joint business venture. They cover how we treat each other, how we do our work, and how we serve our customers and clients. We check our performance against them and hold each other accountable for them. Are we perfect at this? No. Do we have lots of growth we still need to do? Yes. But here's the thing: We both understand and honor the power these rules can have in our lives, so we hold them close and try to follow them. We use these simple rules and the tools we are sharing with you to build self-hope in our relationship at all levels—as friends, as colleagues, as business partners, and as wild-eyed radicals who are out to change the world!

CHAPTER 6

"To the question of your life, you are the answer, and to the problems of your life, you are the solution."

~Joe Cordare

After taking you through the steps of Radical Inquiry in chapter 5, we want to make it real. Let us show you.

A Bit of History

As we began this work, we sat down together and launched our own Radical Inquiry. We had been colleagues and partners in exploration in this new field of human systems dynamics for about seven years. During this time we engaged in a number of conversations around simple rules, and for us they became one critical key to understanding group and organizational culture as well as understanding one-to-one relationships.

We thought about additional ways of supporting and furthering the work around simple rules, so we began to forge a partnership to help individuals develop and integrate their own simple rules into their lives. We followed the steps outlined in Chapter 5, with the intention of mapping a new path for our partnership.

The way we have worked together to continue to clarify and enrich the conversation is a perfect example of the iterative nature of this process.

- We learn something new—either we learn it together or we learn it independently—and it comes into the conversation to inform the next round of talk.

- We have new insights about how our ideas are connected.

- We find new resources to fuel our work.

- We move to a higher plane of thinking about our work together.

- As long as we work together, the Radical Inquiry we started will continue—it remains at the heart of our professional relationship.

The following pages outline how we walked through our own Radical Inquiry to develop our simple rules. Note: This is not representative of one conversation. It is, rather, the culmination of many conversations over time that contributed to our work on the day we finally filled in the blanks. Also we decided that the voice in this chapter would be Royce's as the recorder of a shared process. This was by common consent because she wrote the first draft of this chapter in her own voice, and it resonated with us. We hope it resonates with you, as well.

Step 1 – Define Your Current Pattern

1. **Identify** your current life patterns. Think about what your current patterns are and what they bring you.

2. **Ask** trusted others how they characterize or describe you in the area of life you choose as your focus.

3. **Start** keeping a journal or go back and look through your current journal to see what patterns you can see.

4. **Consider** your behaviors in areas relative to the one you choose to focus on—and on areas that might not seem related.

Mallary and I spent time over a number of months talking about our own patterns of work—alone and with others—and life—alone and with others. We talked about what we saw in each other and what we believed we each brought to this partnership.

Mallary is the more dynamic of the two of us. She travels more and has had a more diverse set of work experiences than I. She has an MBA and a Ph.D., and has been CEO of organizations. Her work experiences include working with people in non-profits, corporate settings, government agencies, and the military. She is an avid reader and can call forth names and models and theories, as needed, at the drop of a hat.

On the other hand, I am more "in my head" than she is. I think I spend more time exploring new ideas and concepts and applying them in new ways. I have a more focused work experience—almost exclusively in public education at all levels and non-profits, with some consulting in other government agencies. I, too, like to read relevant books and articles, but don't retain names and models and theories in the same way Mallary does.

In our personal and home lives we see similarities and differences, as well. She grew up in New York City—I grew up (mostly) in rural Texas. She has one brother; I have three sisters. She has been married for over 35 years; I divorced after 10 years. We both have two grown children who are about the same ages—she raised a boy and a girl; I raised two girls.

In those areas where we don't stand in the same place politically and spiritually, we can still see each other's positions from where we are. As we explored our shared Radical Inquiry, however, we came to realize how similar our desired states were. We came to realize that we have a number of values in common, we see the world in similar ways, and we want similar patterns in our partnership.

We want to generate patterns of learning and growth, honesty and integrity, and intentionality and accountability. We want to build networks and connections that reach across miles and differences to establish sustainable patterns of productive, generative engagement. Finally we realize that these patterns are not an end in themselves. We both realize that the world is in constant flux—people change, situations change, needs and resources change.

We know this process takes work; we do not expect the new patterns we generate to maintain themselves. Both Mallary and I have accepted the responsibility to consider these patterns in all our work together. We agree to use them as a guide to amplify patterns that contribute to what we want and to damp activities and patterns that pull us away from our goals.

These conversations about our own individual and shared patterns was interesting--at various times it was surprising, delightful, challenging, and funny.

Step 2 – Define the Patterns You Want

What is it you really want in life and what are the patterns of behavior and interaction that will get you there?

1. **Draw** three overlapping circles to form a Venn diagram like the one below. In the center, where all three circles overlap, put the one or two words that most clearly describe what it is you want.

2. **Answer** the question in the top circle, "Who are you?" in the context of what you want. This question really is about what draws you in or would hold you in this area of life. What is it? or How is it you want to be in this area of life?

3. **Put** a descriptor of "What is important to you?" in the lower left circle. What is the critical factor or concept related to the idea that will influence your decisions?

4. **Answer** the question "How do you want to connect with others?" in the lower right circle.

As Mallary and I got to the heart of what we wanted to create together, we realized that the most important ideas to each of us are to act intentionally—planfully, creatively, and expansively—in such a way that we contribute to the world in positive and productive ways. We each want to leave a legacy of positive influence in our own local worlds as well as in the world at large. So after consideration, we put "Legacy: Intention and Action" in the center of our Venn diagram.

Next we spent time thinking about the ways we are linked together, in general and specifically in this venture. We know we share a number of like containers—friendship, motherhood, professional life, our roles as Associates at the Human Systems Dynamics Institute, and our shared intellectual pursuits, among others. In this venture, we believe the concept of "radical inquiry to develop simple rules" is the major idea that holds us together. The organizational structures we plan to establish contribute to the landscape of that container as well. So if either of us were called on to respond to the question, "Who are we inside this shared vision?" we would both be able to describe this one set of ideas that binds us together.

Next we began to consider what is important to us in this partnership. We agreed on the ideas of intent and impact. "Intent" for us means first that we want to focus our work—take actions that will purposefully move us toward our goals. Also it represents what we want to enable others to do—use simple rules to focus their own lives and to live inside their own intentions.

"Impact" says that we want our actions to mean something. We will weigh our options and make our decisions based on the impact they may or may not have in the world. Again this also speaks to the ways in which we want to support others in designing the ways they impact the world.

Finally in the third circle, we talked about how we want to connect to others. We both were very clear that we want to be present to our families, colleagues, and clients—and to our reading audience. We want to reach out to you and be real in your lives as well. That is what drives the more conversational, casual tone of this book, for instance. We believed that a more academic, formal tone would feel too impersonal and less present.

The other way we want to connect to others is to participate with them in their journeys of growth and learning. It's not that we want to live vicariously through others' experiences. Nor do we want to

impose ourselves on others' work. What we mean is that we want to walk alongside others, supporting them in their journeys and being a witness to their growth.

Additionally, we recognize that the simple rules are a part of that connection. They govern our decisions about how to interact, how to participate, and how to be accountable to others.

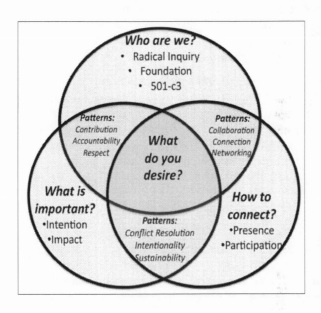

Step 3 – Check Desired Patterns Against the Diagram

Once the Venn diagram is completed, go back and see if the words you put down in the circles work together to create the patterns you said you want.

We went back and reviewed the patterns we said we wanted and considered our responses to the three questions in the Venn diagram. We asked ourselves, "If these three questions are designed to generate specific patterns, what patterns will be generated by our responses?" So we spent some time thinking about these questions.

- *If we look for intention and impact in our work around the simple rules, what patterns will be generated? (This represents the merging of the top and lower left circle of our Venn Diagram.) We believe that generating simple rules in such a frame will generate patterns of individual accountability and carefulness in decision making and action.*

- *If we connect through participation and are present to our families, colleagues, clients and audience as we focus on the simple rules and the venues where we want to share them, what patterns will emerge? (This is the overlap between the top and lower right circles of our Venn diagram.) We believe that people will increase their personal connections by networking and collaborating with others and that we can support and amplify those patterns.*

- *If we focus on participating with others and being present with them in intentional ways that impact their lives in positive directions, what patterns will be generated? (This represents the merging of the lower left and lower right circles on the Venn diagram.) We believe that people will engage together in ways that are authentic, reciprocal, and fair. They will resolve conflict and honor their differences. And they will act intention to sustain more productive and generative relationships.*

Step 4 – Write Your Simple Rules and Test Them

Now you are ready to write your simple rules. Ask yourself, "What are the 5–7 broad rules you could write that would, if you followed them, shape your behavior according to the descriptors you have written? Start by writing a rule for each of the circles. There are some things you need to remember about simple rules.

- Keep the list short. You cannot focus or remember more than 5–7 rules at a time.

- Keep the rules simple. None of them should have lots of qualifiers or "ifs, ands, or buts" in them.

- Start each rule with a verb and make it a positive statement. Always say what you need to do, rather than what not to do. You want the rules to tell you how to act or what to do. It's not enough just to tell you what not to do.

- Remember that the simple rules should be both generalizable and scalable.

Here are the rules Mallary and I came up with.

- ***Sustain the whole, the part, and the greater whole.***
  Human systems dynamics is established on a fundamental belief in open systems. Such a system exists on many levels—intrapersonal, personal, interpersonal, and group. At any point of focus for me, one level describes where I am (whole), one level describes a smaller piece (part), and a third level describes the larger entity of which I am a part (greater whole).

  In real life, using the concept of integrity, this speaks to the fact that I have to work to have integrity in my own thinking and actions (part), and I seek integrity in my partnerships, friendships, and other relationships (whole). Additionally it means that I work toward and support integrity in the local community. I expect and contribute to integrity even at a national and global level (greater whole).

Sustainability at any one level is not possible unless there is some level of sustainability at all three levels. We are too interdependent in human systems to believe that we can ignore the sustainability and health at any level. If individuals are not healthy, the family is not. If families are not healthy, the community cannot be fully healthy. If the communities are blighted, the nation cannot sustain over time.

We believe this simple rule provides a foundation for reminding us to pay attention to patterns that are beyond just our partnership. In our individual work and together we want to move toward sustainability. We want to help our clients sustain their work toward more integrated and balanced lives. But what good is that individual (part) work or the partnered (whole) work if relationships and growth of our own communities and workplaces, even at a national level, are not sustainable? That requires that we pay attention to, contribute to, and vote for those ideals we believe will make this way of life sustainable.

- *Be kind and just.*
  This idea builds on the concept of whole, part, and greater whole. Justice emerges in a society or community when people are treated fairly. No one group experiences privilege simply because of some arbitrary trait or characteristic. People must have access they need to assure their own sustainability as well as that of their families and communities.

106

Being kind and just supports sustainability across scales.

Mallary and I believe that the only privilege an individual should be granted would be a function of his or her own humanity. Children are granted greater consideration because they are more vulnerable. Individuals who are ill or aged may require greater consideration due to their conditions of life. People who have disabilities may require different access, but they have the right to access. It is an individual's condition that should determine how he or she is served by the greater community.

We think of kindness and justice as treating others with fairness and respect, being thoughtful in all our interactions, and assuring access to those shared opportunities. Our actions—in our work and in our daily lives—should be planned and carried out to support this perspective. It is our intention to carry out our partnership in this way, and this simple rule was written to remind us to do so.

- ***Act with intention.***
  Often we float through life, allowing the pressures of each day to frame our direction and activity. We move from one month to the next, accomplishing just what must be done, staying about as busy as we want to be, and checking items off the list as we go along.

  There's nothing wrong with that, and many people live that life. The challenge comes when other goals and accomplishments call us to act beyond a daily plan. Those other goals and accomplishments require us to see past the day-to-day commitments and clarify our intentions to bring about something more. We are then called on to act within those intentions to create the extraordinary.

Sometimes the extraordinary thing we do is to be the best Cub Scout Den Mother or soccer coach. Sometimes extraordinary means being a good parent, partner, or friend. On the other hand, that extraordinary act may produce a best seller or the cure for a dreaded disease or bring about world peace. The point is not the size of impact, the point is that an individual sets a specific goal, acts with focus and intent to reach that outcome, and manifests that reality in his or her own life and in the lives of others.

We think of acting with intention as the force that brings us to write about simple rules, to offer workshops and retreats focused on inquiry and simple rules, and to coach individuals and groups in developing and using simple rules. We believe in the crucial value of simple rules and reinforce each other when we act with intention to promote those concepts. We believe that this simple rule compels us to use the other simple rules to move us toward our goals.

- ***Know yourself.***
  This simple rule is about personal honesty and a commitment to understand your own motivations, fears, hopes, and needs first. It is about knowing what makes you tick, so you can interact with the greater whole more honestly and productively.

  "Know yourself" requires that you recognize your own patterns of decision making and interaction. This means knowing the conditions you set to create patterns, the steps you take to amplify specific patterns, and how you dump others. Know yourself requires an iterative process of Radical Inquiry,

108

continuously examining personal patterns and finding steps to create more productive approaches to living.

We have to recognize and own up to our individual humanness and limitations, and we have to stand proud and offer the world our gifts. Mallary and I have an agreement that we don't hide behind our personal flaws and challenges. Nor do we hoard our gifts. We each individually and as partners know what we offer the world and what we ask in return.

- **Connect with others.**
  Connection is a human need. Yet how often do we go in and out of multiple contacts with people without really connecting on a level that has any meaning at all? For us, it's as though we go onto automatic pilot, greeting people, asking questions, responding to queries, taking care of the basic busyness of the moment without really seeing or hearing the human beings who stand before us.

  This is another example of acting with intention. This simple rule calls us to be intentional in our interactions. Considering the needs and feelings of others, sharing ourselves genuinely, and engaging people in authentic and caring ways are all part of connecting with others. It's not about being the "Chatty Cathy," who is the current center of attention. Nor it is about striking up philosophical conversations with everyone you meet on the street. This simple rule is about being present and available to others, even as you reach out and ask for what you need from those who can and will support you.

  In our work, we think of this simple rule as a way of reminding us that we need to connect with each other—exploring ideas, expanding our understanding, and pushing the boundaries. We also need to find ways to speak to our audiences—through this book, through our workshops, and through the website. And a large responsibility in that is to find ways to be engaging, even when we don't have face-to-face access; to be honest, even when we want to hide our humanity; and to be present with others as they learn and practice new skills.

- *Stand up.*
  This could be said in myriad ways: "Be proactive." "Keep it moving." "Speak up." We chose this way to say it because it implies action and forward movement as well as strength and solidity. We also chose it as a metaphor because we know that there are individuals for whom literally "standing up" is not possible. Regardless of physical ability, every individual can stand against what is wrong, such as resisting cruelty, injustice, and greed. Simultaneously we can all stand for what we believe in and what we count as important.

  Another way people stand up is to own their strengths and accountabilities. They share their gifts, contributing to the greater good. They take accountability for their decisions and their actions.

  When we talk about standing up, we mean that we will support each other in moving this work into the larger world, helping people create and use simple rules to increase the richness in their own lives. It means that we will each, separately and together, stand up and be accountable for our commitments, our actions, and our shortcomings.

Step 5 – Identify One Pattern to Shift, and Plan to Change It

After we decided to work together to produce something about simple rules, we experienced several false starts as we tried to settle on an approach that had meaning to us and felt doable.

Finally we settled on this approach, believing that a more conversational, engaging "how to" book about simple rules would be more useful than any of our earlier plans. At that point, we spent about a week together, outlining the chapters and doing some early drafts of the book. We left at the end of that week, with our individual assignments to finish the writing and to move the foundation and website forward. Unfortunately when we got back to our individual homes, other commitments competed with the time needed for writing.

We generated a pattern of touching base regularly by phone and email to complete the next steps. Neither of us completed our assignments before the first phone call, whereupon we both apologized and forgave each other. We knew how busy we were; we understood how other obligations and deadlines got in the way; we knew that life happens. The result is that we went several months not accomplishing much, and so the book remained unfinished even as we moved months beyond our self-identified publishing timeline.

We decided to change that pattern, get back on schedule and move the processes forward to publish this book, design the journal, create the foundation, finalize the website, and begin training and coaching around simple rules.

As a first step toward changing those patterns, she and I sat down and worked through an Adaptive

Action Cycle to identify specific steps to dump our unproductive patterns and to amplify our productive patterns. Our conversation about this process is documented below.

1. **What? – Look carefully at all the patterns you've identified relative to the issue you choose to address.**

   We examined the information we had about the impact of those patterns over time.

   - *We were more than five months behind in our schedule.*

   - *We both felt guilty and embarrassed at our lack of progress.*

   - *We were both still committed to the project, in spite of having allowed it to lapse.*

   - *We had, in fact, both accomplished significant work in the interim, continuing to learn and gain insights that could enrich this work.*

2. **So What? – Analyze all the information you've collected to determine its meaning in your situation.**

   We knew that we would not complete this book; nor would we reap the benefits of the business activities we pursued if we did not change our patterns.

   - *We needed to find ways to hold ourselves and each other accountable to our agreed-upon shared commitments.*

   - *We needed to be sure to cut ourselves some slack and either get busy or quit feeling guilty and stop beating ourselves up for not doing the work.*

- *We needed to get specific about the agreements and work and do what needed to be done; setting deadlines and engaging others for help with accountability.*

3. **Now What? – Identify your strategies to shift the conditions so that the patterns will change, put those strategies into action, and see what happens.**

We agreed on the following strategies, using the Venn diagram from our Radical Inquiry to talk about how to set the conditions for us to build the patterns we wanted.

Who are we?

We still believed in the concept and agreed that this was the right "container" for our work. Our only strategy in this area was to remap the steps that needed to be taken as we moved toward the goals we set.

What's important around here?

We agreed to act with more intention—to maintain this work as a priority and move forward with the action steps that needed to be done.

We agreed to support each other's intentions by recognizing and responding to our individual and shared accountabilities and commitments.

Additionally we talked about impact. We took time to recognize the impact of our feelings of guilt and apology when we were not carrying out the work. Those negative feelings had too much potential to interfere with our overall working relationship and this work in particular. We also talked about the impact of not completing our work: Loss or postponement of a valuable tool for individuals; lost chances to expand the field of human systems dynamics; lost opportunities for revenue for the organizations we supported as well as for us individually. We agreed to minimize this impact by moving forward and reinforcing the actions we needed to take.

How do we connect?

Most of the strategies we set fit in this area, impacting the other circles. We agreed:

- *to remain aware of the opportunities we were missing as well as the various struggles we were experiencing,*

- *to be more supportive of ourselves and each other by letting go of the guilt and focus on the pleasure of our relationship and the work,*

- *to engage others as participants in the process as reviewers, editors, and sources of feedback, and*

- *to set up regular calls for connecting.*

So that is the process—it's as simple as that; it's as complex as that; it's as rewarding as that. Since you are now reading this book, you know that we were able, finally, to step fully into this Radical Inquiry and use those strategies to stay on track as we finished the manuscript. The even better news is that we completed our mission with only slight adjustments to our new timeline.

The process has not been without glitches. The world didn't change to a gentle rosy hue that made everything smooth. The manuscript didn't magically appear on our computer screens, suddenly finished and ready for publication. We did, however, work through our strategies, returning to the simple rules to help us stay focused, and sticking to our timelines to keep us moving forward, and returning to the goals.

The remainder of this chapter is a blank form for you to use in your own Radical Inquiry. You can accomplish this in a number of ways. You may wish to create your own personal simple rules and set your own goals. Or you might engage someone else in working through a partnership. Or you may want to try using our form to create simple rules with your family, with colleagues, or among a larger group in your community.

Use our example. Remember that, while we provide guidelines and suggestions, what is right is what works for you. Good luck, and as you complete your work, visit our website at

www.simplerulesfoundation.org

Please feel free to get in touch with us for further suggestions, hints, coaching, and support.

Radical Inquiry: Change My Life

Today, _____, 20__,

I set my intention and begin a process to change my life, stepping into this Radical Inquiry to explore, examine, understand, and take action to influence patterns in my life relative to _____.

(name the area you want to work on)

Step 1

What current patterns do I see in my life relative to the area I want to address? List them here.

1. Of those patterns, the area of focus I am choosing is . . .

2. People in my life tell me . . .

3. From my journaling I am aware that . . .

4. As I look at other areas relative to this, I see . . .

5. I have also discovered this about patterns in my life...

Step 2

What are the patterns I want in my life, relative to this area of interest? What do I want, and what will get me there? Feel free to fill this page with your brainstormed ideas.

What picture describes the patterns I want?

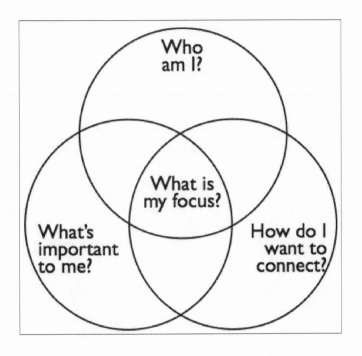

Step 3

In what ways do my desired patterns match what I described in the Venn diagram?

1. When I consider "Who am I?" in light of "What's important to me?" what patterns do I think will emerge?

2. When I consider "Who am I?" in light of "How do I want to connect?" what patterns do I think will emerge?

3. When I consider, "What's important to me" in light of "How do I want to connect?" what patterns do I think will emerge?

4. How do these patterns compare to the patterns I said I wanted in Step 2?

Step 4

What simple rules will help me create the patterns I want?

1. What is (at least) one simple rule that addresses "Who am I?"

2. What is (at least) one simple rule that addresses "What's important to me?"

3.   What is (at least) one simple rule that addresses "How do I want to connect?"

4.   What other rules might help me form the patterns I want?

5. Do my simple rules fit the format and "rules" for simple rules?

6. Here are the ways each of my simple rules is **generalizable** across all areas of my life:

Personal Life:

Community Life:

Work Life:

Social Life:

Volunteer or Faith Community Life:

Other Areas:

Here are the ways each of my simple rules is **scalable**...

Personal Life:

Family Life:

Local Community Issues:

National Issues:

Global Issues:

Here is my full list of simple rules.

Step 5
What do I want to work on first?

1. What current data and information do I have about the pattern I want to work on?

2. What meaning can I make from the data and
information I have?

3. What steps can I take to address one of those issues? How long will I commit to try these first steps?

4. Given the steps I am planning to take, what differences do I think I can count on? How will I measure them?

5. Now that I have met my initial commitment on these strategies, what do I need to do next? Continue these strategies and begin to move toward the next challenge? Alter these a bit to change what I am doing?

6. How will I begin to collect information to start on this next phase of my lifelong Radical Inquiry?

CHAPTER 7

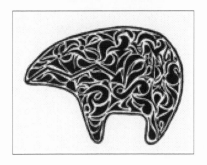

"It is not down in any map; true places never are."
~Herman Melville

In chapter 6 we provided you a glimpse of our own journey of Radical Inquiry to explore, identify, and develop our simple rules. Chapter 7 offers two additional tools to help you implement your simple rules and shift your own patterns.

Across the street and around the globe, people struggle in their attempts to deal with the realities and multiple challenges of a changing world. Circumstances of organizational and communal life are in flux as individuals look for ways to deal with increasing diversity, deal with increased information flow, and reduce carbon footprints and use natural resources more respectfully. The universal search is for new and different ways to manage life's requirements.

It is not surprising, then, that you find yourself redefining traditional notions, beliefs, and ideas. Where you once had all the answers, you find that much of what has worked in the past no longer seems viable or even relevant. Individuals, families, corporations, communities, and cultures find that much beyond the most immediate future seems unclear and unpredictable. Society is experiencing grave challenges around seeing and maintaining the signal fires that worked in the past.

Even if your own ship is on course, you may sometimes wonder if the world is just a bit out of joint. Like when you sit down in your favorite restaurant and the table is unsteady on its legs. It wobbles back and forth beneath you until you take a couple of napkins, fold them into a small square and wedge it under the base. With that one act, you exerted influence and steadied a situation. Now you can relax and enjoy your meal.

Sometimes it's an unsteady table; sometimes it's a chair faced into the sun; sometimes it's a time out, a do-over, an apology, a re-boot or coming to a conclusion. Just imagine if everyone everywhere took a moment to fold a napkin. What if someone pulled out a pen and paper to map out an answer? What if gestures, deeds, words, or moments of silence were used to connect? What if people began to seek ways to shift their perspectives to better accomplish their work?

Each of those acts would lead to others; each individual light of connection could lead to another, and to the next and the next and the next ... leading eventually to a path of possibility and hope. Each individual light could be the difference that makes a difference to brighten individual and collective paths toward changing the world.

Just Do Something

Why is it important that you take action? Why does it matter whether you shift your situation? It is because your individual action is at the core of the

change this book is about. It is because your individual action is about changing the patterns in your own life, and you are a part of this greater complex system called humanity. Each person is tied inextricably—sometimes in ways that are both small and large; sometimes in single connections and sometimes multiple ones—to worldwide patterns of hope and despair; of productivity and barrenness; of peace and conflict; of sustainability and waste. In the midst of these polarities, many individuals and groups want to create patterns that satisfy important social and personal needs—and local choices can yield global impacts.

We believe this process we have shared can help set the conditions that have the best chance of generating necessary patterns. We begin by asking three questions.

- Who am I?

- What is important to me?

- How to I want to connect with others?

A sustainable future depends on significant shifts in values, culture, and structure toward patterns that enable us to be more sensitive to our environments, more responsive to challenges and opportunities, and more resilient in the face of change. These patterns can only exist at the community, organizational, national or global levels if they exist at the individual level. Each of us generates patterns that contribute to whatever happens at those larger scales.

In other words, establishing patterns that enable that level of sustainability depends upon you. Many people seek better and faster responses and action steps to address situations and resolve problems. How fortunate that you are not alone. You can participate in this process and find your own voice. You can embrace a sense of ownership and recognize the power you have within your environment. Light the next signal fires for others who seek this path as well.

In the last chapter we talked about identifying one pattern you want to change and what you can do to change it. Sometimes just setting the course is not enough. You need tools and support to maintain new patterns.

The Simple Plan: Each One of Us

As you have seen, it was through a thoughtful and exciting process that we discovered and distilled our own simple rules. We offer these to you as an example of how we demonstrate our commitment to ongoing learning, growth, and self-organization. By thinking about simple rules in this way, we also define the standard by which we measure them, articulate them internally and externally, and act accordingly.

There is no trick here. Once you have answered your three critical questions of *Who are you? What is important to you?* and *How do you want to connect with others?*—in other words set the conditions—you begin to learn more about yourself and what you need to do to establish and build self-hope. We offer additional tools to help you as they have helped us.

Building Sustainable Patterns

We used a set of tools to define our shared simple rules in creating this book and in our partnership around this work. Our simple rules are:

- Sustain the whole, the part and the greater whole.
- Be kind and just.
- Act with intention.

- Know yourself.

- Connect with others.

- Stand up.

One thing you will realize as you develop your own simple rules is that while they might sometimes seem at cross-purposes, they are most often massively entangled with each other. Look at our list. How can you act with intention if you don't know yourself? You really do have to connect with others to sustain the whole, the part, and the greater whole.

If you think about what simple rules are and where they come from, this only makes sense. Simple rules set the conditions for the patterns you want to generate. They create coherence and continuity, so they are, by their very nature, going to overlap.

At the same time, you may find instances when your simple rules seem to contradict each other. For instance, what if we spend so much time connecting with others that we don't have time or energy left for levels of self-reflection that help us to act with intention? Life is full of unexplainable possibilities and seeming contradictions; the best we can hope for is to be able to appreciate and negotiate ambiguities and surprises as they emerge.

You may have noticed by now that the simple rules really aren't simple. They are relatively easy to identify, once you know what patterns you want, and they are short and simple to state. They are not, however, simple to execute in life. You have to consider their impact. What do they really mean? How will our behavior change?

It is not enough merely to state simple rules, you have to understand in real, concrete terms what they actually mean in day-to-day interactions. How will they manifest themselves in your life and how will they be used? We used the Legacy Sustainability

Model to explore this question because of its broad application to the ways we are embedded in the network of relationships around us. Think about how each of the elements of the model can help you create and sustain your simple rules and the patterns.

Warning: It could get way too complicated to be useful if you tried to take every single simple rule and describe an interaction for every element of the Legacy Sustainability Model. We recommend you use this list of elements as a general screen in your thinking about the ways your simple rules can and will impact your behavior.

- Communications
- Continuous Assessment
- Connections
- Constructs
- Coherence
- Commitments
- Capacity Building

The additional tools listed here help you make sense of your simple rules and other insights from the Radical Inquiry. You may want to return to them often to establish and reinforce the greatest impact on your own life.

Knowing and Doing

This tool helped us articulate answers to questions about how the rules might manifest themselves in our lives. This allows you to shift from theoretic simple rules to more concrete applications and the actions you can take. Using this reflective process makes your own rules real to you.

Here's how it works. Write down your own simple rules. Underneath each simple rule, make two lists with the headings of *Knowing* and *Doing*. In the *Knowing* column, write three or four statements that describe what that rule means to you. In the second column, *Doing*, write three or four specific examples of how that rule will change or influence your actions.

Below is an example of what our lists look like, using two of our simple rules.

Simple rule:
Sustain the whole, the part, and the greater whole.

Knowing

- Our planning incorporates and considers our needs for those of others in our lives, our communities, and society.

- We share our learning and contribute to others' learning, growth, and development.

- Our actions ripple throughout our lives, and we influence the world in large and small ways, some of which we may never know.

Doing

- Ensure that messages are clear, open and two-way.

- Engage in honest and authentic give and take with family and community.

- Seek and share input and perspectives.

- Support research and practice of HSD and pursue knowledge development, dissemination, and integration; support new patterns and learning for others.

- Measure progress in multiple ways.

Simple Rule:
Be kind and just.

Knowing

- Justice is access and allowing each individual the privilege of his or her humanity.

- Kindness is respectfulness in word and action.

- Power is about influence and is not limited. Grant and generate voice in interaction with others.

Doing

- Engage in open, authentic give and take.

- Act with compassion and thought. Support and drive the best in ourselves and others.

- Recognize and support opportunities to influence the world around us.

- Understand the boundaries and constraints of privilege in our own lives.

Strategy Criteria

So now you know the patterns you want to create in your life. You know what simple rules will help to generate those patterns, and you have even begun to think about the kinds of behavior you will need to pursue to live those simple rules out. What is next?

Now is the time to develop your own personal strategic plan. That may sound a bit too formal or official for personal use, but we don't think so. Strategic planning is just another way of mapping the strategies for moving toward what you want.

Strategy is about making decisions and taking action—for the purpose of achieving goals and ensuring survival. In fact, if we plan carefully, paying

attention to the patterns in life and to the ways we can sustain those patterns we find desirable, then success will move us beyond mere survival. We will move toward a higher level of functioning and fitness.

Strategy, when used as a part of our Radical Inquiry, is also about generating a unique and valuable stance. We stated it earlier in the book, but this is a good time to reiterate the critical importance of engaging in this work from a position of inquiry. You bring unique perspectives and questions to your own strategies, and that unique perspective means you alone will see your specific answers. Don't try to predict or control. Step into your strategies with an open mind. Embrace surprise; look for the unknown.

Developing strategy from this stance of inquiry reduces uncertainty. Remember, control is only a fond illusion, and the only power you have in planning lies in your real ability to influence patterns. You can and do shift those patterns every day with every act (or inaction).

When we develop strategies based on our questions about what can and will move us toward greater fitness, we open generative paths of communication and find the best use of physical, emotional, and temporal resources. Strategy provides a framework upon which we can make decisions that influence our life patterns in positive and productive ways.

Michael Porter identifies four primary criteria for strategy. Each of his criteria is relevant and applicable in strategizing your personal Radical Inquiry.

- **Strategy rests on differences and what is unique about you.** The patterns of our lives are similarities, differences, and relationships that have meaning across space and time. Patterns enable learning, movement, and growth when we remain open to possibility and new insights that come with inquiry.

Our simple rules and inherent strategy start with the truth that each of us is unique and moves toward fitness as we respond and move forward in intentional ways. Our strategies help us navigate the differences we encounter to find results that fit our own uniqueness.

- **There are trade-offs.** It is a fact of life that we must give in order to receive; contribute in order to reap; and in every decision, action, and circumstance, we use the Adaptive Action Cycle to respond—whether we realize that's what we are doing or not. We capture our data, figure out what it means in our current situation, and make choices about how best to respond to opportunities, events, and barriers in our environments. The nature of choice is that we must accept some things and reject others. In all of our lives there are the gives-to-gets. What are we ready and willing to give, donate, contribute, turn in, provide, and offer in order to find, understand, become, perceive, catch, and grasp that which we value? This question of trade-off and personal value lies at the heart of the inquiry stance as we explore our worlds, our choices, and our opportunities.

- **There must be fit.** Fitness is possible once you have clarity about who you are, what is important to you, and how you want to connect to others. Are you in that place? Is your radical stance of inquiry authentic, meaningful, and consistent with your values, goals, and vision? Have you thoughtfully set the conditions to create new patterns in your life? Strategies that are aligned move us forward powerfully and authentically.

- **Continually rediscover yourself.** We exist in real time and space and are subject to influences of day-to-day shifts that may occur. Because we are open to outside forces, we respond to the greater system we see as our environment. Do I take the raincoat

and umbrella or do I keep my fingers crossed it will not rain? Do I walk under the ladder or am I too superstitious to take the chance? We learn and grow constantly. With each alteration and iteration, we evolve. Our task is to pay attention, rediscover ourselves, and remain true to our spirit and core. If we do not include strategies to learn and grow and continue to seize what is revealed on our journey, we are indeed doomed.

Remember, strategists operate in a world of uncertainty and complexity—just as we do—and their job is to design a coherent and productive path through that landscape. That work takes courage, and what distinguishes strategists from others is that they will act when others will not—just as we must! The following list reflects our simple rules through the lens of these criteria. Again we have included only two examples here.

Strategy criteria (Simple Rule):
Sustain the whole, the part, and the greater whole.

Differentiation

- How am I both independent and interdependent within my environment?

- What is it that separates me from others; connects me to others?

Fit

- How will a shift in behavior support my goals around sustainability, quality of life, and social justice?

- Are my new patterns coherent and consistent with my beliefs?

Trade-Offs

- How does this inquiry help me choose best options?
- What do I gain/lose as my priorities change?

Rediscover Yourself

- What new opportunities for growth are appearing?.
- How do I support my new patterns and behaviors?
- What are the similarities; what are the differences?

Strategy criteria (Simple Rule): Be kind and just.

Differentiation

- What are the differences that make a difference?
- How have my local actions shifted patterns in my greater world?

Fit

- How does this new pattern align with my environment, my family, and my community?
- How do my behaviors contribute to authenticity and my place in the world?

Trade-Offs

- Where can I be most effective?
- What "gives-to-gets" do I experience when I try to support others and their patterns?

Rediscover Yourself

- How can I continue to learn about who I am as I clarify my place in the world, based on relationships with others?
- What patterns can I develop to support new ways of seeing myself in the world?

Here is a final note about strategy. Developing and working through strategy is a reflective process. As our strategies unfold, we have work to do. Strategies are not just tasks ... they are not just disparate action steps—neither whimsical nor random. A strategy refers to a whole operation or set of activities aimed at one goal or outcome. So even when we develop strong strategies that meet all four strategic criteria, there has to be some understanding of the greater picture and how each step shifts the environment and influences the next.

Personal strategic planning is a meaningful and evocative process that calls you to reflect on your goals and focus on your values. Remember that good questions lead to new questions, so the journey is not over. What's left is for you to develop a strategy, make a commitment to act—and then ACT!

Conclusion

As we look around and wonder if society has "outstretched" traditional models and paradigms about how we can live in the world, we stop and think. There is hope.

Processes we use to recognize and appreciate differences, shared relationships, and interdependence between and among people around us allow for greater coherence, progress, and common ground. Shifting to a definition of power as "ability to influence" allows people to respond and collaborate more effectively. Co-existence and co-evolution help us deal with the turbulence and uncertainty of what's ahead. Learning to negotiate our very significant differences enables us to manage and resolve conflict in ways that strengthen spirit, foster interdependence, and support creativity.

Our plan is not to take over the world; it is to empower you to shift your patterns and create your own simple rules to live a purposeful life. And we have offered a series of tools and approaches to support you in creating your own signal fires along that journey.

See what lies beyond these tools to support you in your lifelong Radical Inquiry.

Chapter 8

"A small group of thoughtful people could change the world. Indeed, it's the only thing that ever has."
~Margaret Mead

"In union there is strength."

~Aesop

"Sticks in a bundle are unbreakable."
~Kenyan Proverb

Each of these quotes communicates the purpose of this final chapter. We invite you to become a part of a movement—to join us in changing the world, as each of us contributes what we can.

Get Active

Simple rules are all about action ... taking steps to move toward a sustainable, productive life. You have used Radical Inquiry to go deep into who you are and create your own simple rules. Now it's time to to take action.

As a result of beginning this journey, you will begin to see patterns everywhere you look: your behaviors, distractions, responses, facial expressions, thought processes, doodling on paper, career choices ... they all create the patterns of life. It is our hope that you will want to talk about them, sharing your observations, insights, and ideas with people around you. It is our hope that you will share those patterns with us and others who have read and benefitted from this book.

Simple rules work for individuals and for groups —anywhere humans live, work, or play together in families, teams, communities, or organizations. They help people establish coherence in groups that are just launching, and they are helpful to groups that have been functioning for awhile and yet still need to increase their shared productivity. Simple rules can work for book clubs, congregations, little league teams, and classrooms.

Once you realize the power of simple rules and the Radical Inquiry process, you will see endless possibilities in your own life. It is our hope that you will connect with others to share your questions, your stories, your successes, and your insights about the role and power of simple rules in your every day life.

First

Look for simple rules in every arena of life.

Are you getting prepared for your first classroom teaching assignment? How about these?

- Teach and learn in every interaction.
- Actively listen and respond to others' voices.
- Honor individuality and differences.
- Promote equity, respect, and fairness.
- Help sustain the world around us.
- Explore the unknown with enthusiasm, wonder, and integrity.

Are you planning to run for political office? How about these?

- Support health, well-being, safety, and security.
- Engage the community.
- Create a sense of belonging.
- Practice and promote social justice.
- Stand up for diversity and inclusion.
- Do no harm.

> **_Are you considering launching a new business? How about these?_**
>
> - Maintain sensible and consistent financial growth.
> - Consider the company; consider the environment
> - Serve ethically and effectively.
> - Innovate, learn, and sustain with quality.
> - Act globally with integrity and compassion

> **_Are you working to raise your children and build a strong family? How about these?_**
>
> - Treat each other with respect and fairness.
> - Listen with an open mind and open heart.
> - Teach and learn with love and joy.
> - Sustain each others' health, safety, and security, whether we are together or apart.
> - Recognize and appreciate our differences.

The thing about Simple Rules is this: you can explore them, collect them, play with them, revise them, shout them out, live them. That is their gift. They help us explore our lives as we play with ideas and share with each other. They provide an anchor in our decisions and actions. They become a point of negotiation and discussion about who we are individually and as a group.

One final tool we offer is, **Radical Inquiry Journal**, a companion piece for this book to help you on your journey.

Second

Unlike countless categories and approaches that are out there in the stratosphere for self-help, we are offering you something else: **Self-Hope**.

Do you know about hope? It's that feeling that what we want, need or aspire to will turn out for the best. It is about expectations, looking forward to something with confidence and competence. It is the capacity to believe or trust that what we wish for will come to pass.

Self-hope is the radical place you stand when you set the conditions in your life to support your new patterns. It is entirely about

• Who you are;

• What is important to you; and

• How you want to connect to others.

Your mission, should you decide to accept it, is all about you. Are you ready to create the self you want and the world you want to live in?

Third and Final

We believe the way to a sustainable future is through simple rules that support adaptation and growth, and our plan is to let loose simple rules on the world.

We have created the Simple Rules Foundation as a call to action for those of you who want to get actively involved and would like the world around you to be different. The Foundation will provide a conduit for collecting, disseminating, contributing, and integrating simple rules into and throughout our lives and our world—sharing stories and measuring how we are doing in creating a dent in the universe.

We care about the world, and we care about you. We want you to discover the self-hope in your life— we want you to join us in creating and populating a world where hope is more than a wish. We want you to join us in a world where hope is an abundant resource, available to everyone! And you are the key because you are one in a million.

- You are **One In A Million** individuals who want to share the sounds of their voices—to be part of and contribute to a conversation that is greater than they are.

- You are **One In A Million** individuals who want to reach out to others to connect in new and broader ways. Now, more than ever before in history, we have the means and resources to do that.

- You are **One In A Million** individuals who want to be part of a group working in a common cause toward a shared and meaningful goal.

That is what it means to participate in this global effort to create Self-Hope. It is simply opening your door, your heart, and your mind to share the possibilities in your everyday life. It is a quest to bring that openness to people around the world.

We invite you to be part of this quest. We hope you will join us in lighting signal fires around the world to bring others to share in this journey with us. To build a world where signal fires of hope guide

each of us as we continue to grow, adapt, create, learn, and evolve.

Simple rules are more than just a good idea. Self-hope is not simply a "do-over," where we just commit the same old mistakes, but a way to re-invent our approaches to both the large and the small events and opportunities in our lives.

Now think about events and opportunities that build hope in the world.

• Riding the wave of pride following a Presidential election no one ever believed was possible

• Rolling up your sleeves and rebuilding a community destroyed by natural disaster

• Going back to school for a second, volunteer career

• Launching a global initiative to meet the needs of the present without compromising the ability of future generations to meet their own needs

Look at each of these events through the lens of simple rules. Discern new and more coherent patterns. Envision yourself as the individual, in the context of the whole and the greater whole: constructing, shifting, contributing, forming a coalition, speaking with others in one voice, standing up, holding out your hands, and being a part of an empowered force to be reckoned with. Come on and grab hold!

We believe in people. We think they want to share the sound of their own voices—and truly want to be part of and contribute to a conversation that is greater than they are.

People want to reach out to others. They want to connect in new and broader ways. *Now, more than ever before in history, they have the means and resources to do that.* Finally, we believe that people want to be part of a group working in a common cause toward a shared and meaningful goal.

What does it mean to attend and participate in this global effort to create Self-Hope? It is about the true and useful: ideas, application, learning, growth, connection, peace. We'd like to invite you to be part of it and here is how you take that first step toward joining us.

Imagine your most desired future: Imagine it is 5, 10, or 20 years from now. Look around you and imagine what you see. What is your neighborhood like? What are your children doing? What are you doing that creates meaning in your life? In other words:

- What kind of world do you want?

- What are you going to do to create that world?

- Now start the conversation.

We state this once again: self-hope is simply opening your door, your heart, and your mind to the myriad possibilities in your everyday life. We are on a quest to bring that openness to people around the world.

Conclusion

We invite you to be part of this quest. We hope you will join us in lighting signal fires around the world to connect with others and bring them along. To build a sustainable, productive world where signal fires of hope guide each of us as we continue to grow, adapt, create, learn, and evolve.

SELECTED RESOURCES

Be sure to look for the accompanying tool that goes with this book:
Radical Inquiry Journal,
A Companion Tool for
Simple Rules: A Radical Inquiry into Self.

Bar-Yam, Yaneer. *Concepts in Complex Adaptive Systems*. New England Complex Systems Institute 2007 [cited. Available from http://necsi.edu/guide/concepts/.]

Eoyang, Glenda H. 1997. *Coping with Chaos: Seven Simple Tools*. Circle Pines, MN: Lagumo.

Eoyang, Glenda H., ed. 2003. *Voices from the Field: An Introduction to Human Systems Dynamics*. Circle Pines, MN: Human Systems Dynamics Institute.

Holladay, Royce. 2005. *Legacy: Sustainability in a Complex Human System*. Circle Pines, MN: Human Systems Dynamics Institute.

Holladay, Royce. 2005. "Simple Rules: Organizational DNA." *OD Practitioner* 37 (4).

Holladay, Royce and Kristine Quade. 2009. *Influencing Patterns for Change: a Human Systems Dynamics Primer for Leaders*. Create Space.

O'Connor, Joseph and Ian McDermott. 1997. *The Art of Systems Thinking: Essential Skills for Creativity and Problem Solving*. Thorsons: London.

Olson, Edwin E., and Glenda H. Eoyang. 2001. *Facilitating Organizational Change: Lessons from Complexity Science*. San Francisco: Jossey-Bass/ Pfeiffer.

Porter, Michael E. 1985. *Competitive Advantage: Creating and Sustaining Superior Performance.* New York: The Free Press.

Porter, Michael E. 1996. "What is Strategy?" *Harvard Business Review* (October 1996).

Quade, Kristine and Royce Holladay. 2010. *Dynamical Leadership: Building Adaptive Capacity for Uncertain Times.* Apache Junction, AZ: Gold Canyon Press.

Rogers, Everett M. 1983. *Diffusion of Innovations.* New York: The Free Press.

Sibley, David and Julia Yoshida. 2002. "Spotting Patterns on the Fly." *Harvard Business Review.*

Sweeney, Linda Booth. 2008. *Connected Wisdom: Living Stories about Living Systems.* Hong Kong: Regent Publishing Services Ltd.

Sweeney, Linda Booth. 2001. *When a Butterfly Sneezes.* Waltham, MA: Pegasus Communications.

Tytel, Mallary. 2009. *Vision Driven: Lessons Learned from the e Small Business C-Suite.* Apache Junction, AZ: Gold Canyon Press.

SELECTED
WEBSITES

BOIDS
http://www.red3d.com/cwr/boids/

Human Systems Dynamics Institute
http:/www.hsdinstitute.org

Healthy Workplaces
http:/www.healthyworkplaces.com

Simple Rules
http:/www.simplerules.org

Simple Rules Foundation
http:/www.simplerulesfoundation.org

Generative Engagement
http://patternsandpossibilities.squarespace.com

Vision Driven
http:/wision-driven.net

DOODLE ART FIGURES

I have been drawing these figures for a long time. At first they were a distraction when I would sit in long meetings or when I found myself with nothing to do as I waited for my kids to finish their activities. Over the years, I have shared the images with friends and colleagues. When we started talking about the art for this book, Mallary suggested that we use some of my "doodle art" as illustrations. We selected these figures for the book concepts according to what they represented to us as we thought about each of the chapters. The following descriptions outline what they mean to us.

~Royce Holladay

	The **spiral** is a Celtic symbol for personal growth and learning. It is also used in many ancient belief systems to represent the cycle of living and learning through life. We have used it as the foundation for the book as our symbol for self-hope
	The **circle** stands for completion and wholeness. We chose it for Glenda's foreword because of her holistic perspective and deep insights that created the field of human systems dynamics.

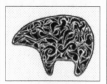	The **bear** represents strength, wisdom, and commitment to the task, which is what that chapter of the book speaks to.
	We used this **tree of life** image to represent the idea of systems and the ways in which they anchor and support our lives.
	The **intertwined circles** reflect the interconnections and relationships of the Radical Inquiry. We chose it to bring to mind the use of the Venn diagram in the Radical Inquiry.
	The **turtle**, having survived for millions of years, represents resilience and adaptation. For this reason we chose it to represent sustainability.
	In spite of its miniature size, to us, the image of the **hummingbird** represents responsiveness in its agility, speed, longevity, and strength. We believe these are characteristics simple rules bring to our lives as well.
	The **Yin and Yang** represents the balance of similarity and difference inherent in the whole. We chose it to reflect the ways we came to balance our skills, perceptions, and insights in the process of writing this book.

 This **signal fire** represents the signal fires we have set and those we invite you to light for yourselves and others as you create your path to new patterns in your life. They are our guideposts and touchstones.

ABOUT THE AUTHORS

Royce Holladay has worked to train, support, and coach individuals in organizations in a variety of settings. Based in her school reform efforts since the early 1990s, Royce focuses on planning for individual performance improvement, organizational leadership, and personal growth at all levels across a system. Her background in strategic leadership and human systems dynamics is a strong foundation for her understanding of individual performance in human systems.

Currently serving as Director of The Network for Human Systems Dynamics Institute, Royce has presented workshops at state, national, and international conferences, and has co-authored three books and numerous articles. As a writer, poet, and artist, she uses stories, images, and down-to-earth descriptions to make complex ideas simple to apply in everyday life.

Mallary Tytel is the president and founder of Healthy Workplaces, a national consulting firm that focuses on supporting individuals and organizations through coaching, training, systems change, and sustainability. Her work in human systems dynamics has provided the foundation for her research-to-practice approach to creating and influencing systems change.

The former CEO of an international non-profit corporation, Mallary has served as a key advisor to senior-level personnel within the U.S. Department of Defense; and has created and delivered innovative systems-based training in over 40 communities worldwide. She has a Ph.D. in Public Health Promotion and Organizational Systems, an M.B.A., and is a certified executive coach and mediator. In her spare time she mentors budding women entrepreneurs.

Made in the USA
Charleston, SC
07 January 2012